Published by
Cleveland Landmarks Press, Inc.
13610 Shaker Boulevard, Suite 503
Cleveland, Ohio 44120-1592
www.clevelandbook.com
(216) 658-4144

©2007 Cleveland Landmarks Press, Inc.
All Rights Reserved

ISBN: 978-0-9367602-4-7

LIBRARY OF CONGRESS NUMBER:
2007936781

Designed by
John Yasenosky, III

Printed by
BookMasters, Inc.
Ashland, Ohio

Dr. James A. Toman

4/13/08

Jim,

Thanks, as always.

JT

surviving the drought:
cleveland sports fans since 1964

For diehard Cleveland fans, it's been that kind of life. *(David Richard photo)*

acknowledgments

Many people provided support and guidance throughout the process of researching and writing this book.

Hearty thanks to Scott Longert and Ann Sindelar at the Western Reserve Historical Society, for their assistance in finding and reproducing key sports photos. In addition, thanks to Bill Barrow and Lynn Duchez, from the special collections of the Cleveland State University Libraries, who located old photos from before 1982.

Many photographers also helped in this effort, and I appreciate their generosity of spirit. Ron Kuntz, David Richard of the Lorain *Morning Journal*, and Karin McKenna provided excellent photographs for the book. I also thank the many other photographers whose work is now housed in the city's various archives; I have identified their contributions wherever possible.

As for interviews, I talked to and emailed more than 200 Cleveland fans, and I thank each one for taking the time to respond thoughtfully to my questions. Especially helpful in these efforts were John "Big Dawg" Thompson and Chris Wagner.

Many thanks also to Jim Donovan, the sports director at WKYC, Terry Pluto of the *Plain Dealer*, and Dan Coughlin, longtime Cleveland sportscaster, currently at WJW.

Cleveland legends also helped provide insights for the book, and I thank in particular Bingo Smith, Dick Shafrath, Kenny Konz, and Sam Rutigliano. Gracious thanks also to Jim Iona and Bill Fritz and the Akron Browns Backers, for helping to set up interviews with some of the Browns' most diehard fans.

Chris Butler helped edit the book, and John Yasenosky superbly designed it, and I appreciate their incredible efforts. I also thank Dan and Kathy Cook, partners in Cleveland Landmarks Press, Inc.

While it pains me to admit it, the constant harassment from my relatives in Pittsburgh, specifically, Tom, Max, and Sean Stockhausen, forced me to finally put to paper what it means to continually cheer for teams that have not seen championships in my lifetime.

Special thanks go to James Toman, whose careful editing and research, helpful guidance, and supportive encouragement meant the world to me during the life of the project.

I am grateful for the love and support of my mother, Marcia Deegan. I have undying appreciation for my father, Tim Deegan. We spent many days and nights cheering Cleveland teams, and those memories were the seeds of this book. Thank you for your love and support.

Finally, I am particularly grateful to my wife Liz, who has had to put up with my rantings as a Cleveland sports fan and who supported me in my vision to finally capture what it means to live and die with every shot, pass, and at-bat in Cleveland sports. Although she is a Pittsburgh fan, her graciousness and assistance meant all the difference in bringing this book to fruition. I certainly could not have done it without her. In addition, Kate, Sydney, and Sam Deegan all provided heartwarming moments for my life which Cleveland teams were unable to do.

To all I acknowledge my debt. This book is a result of real collaboration. Its strengths are due to the generosity of my helpers. The weaknesses are my own.

Gregory G. Deegan
2007

prologue

They are a unique fraternity, Cleveland fans. For no other subculture in the U.S. are the words "next year" more loaded with emotion, hope, desperation, and anticipation. Cleveland fans are a legion of Charlie Browns.

Most people remember the *Peanuts* comic strip by Charles Schulz. Year after year Lucy would invite Charlie Brown to kick the football she was teeing up. And every year, Lucy would pull that ball away just as Charlie was in his kicking approach. The ball would remain in Lucy's grasp, and Charlie would land on his back with a thud. Charlie was appealingly naive. It seems everyone would root that he had learned his lesson, but he never did.

Every year (actually, every game, every snap, every pitch, every tip-off), like Charlie being invited by Lucy, Cleveland fans are encouraged to kick the proverbial football. After years of seeing that pigskin plucked away from under them, they halfheartedly try to convince themselves logically that this time it will be no different. Hope, however, wins out over history, and once again they try to kick that football. Like readers of the *Peanuts* cartoon commiserating with Charlie, even non-Clevelanders, yell to the Cleveland throng, "Don't do it!"

Yet Cleveland fans give it a shot every year. They prime themselves to boot that ball, even though they know at some level that, well, it's going to end just as it always does - without a championship.

While individual teams may eclipse Cleveland's record for years without a championship (like the Chicago Cubs, for instance, or the Detroit Lions), not one of the 47 other major league cities (those that host one or more major league baseball, football, hockey, or basketball teams) can match the 43 years of tumbleweed that has whirled through Cleveland since it won its last major sports championship.

When the clock ticked off the last seconds of the 1964 NFL Championship and the city of Cleveland celebrated the Browns' incredible 27-0 upset of Johnny Unitas and the Baltimore Colts, who could have known that the banner headlines announcing a championship for a Cleveland team in a major sport would be taking a hiatus for over four decades?

Who would have thought that the Cleveland Indians would step out onto the field for 5,977 more games without winning a World Series? Or who could have imagined that the Browns would pad up for 522 more games without once making it to the Super Bowl? In 1964, the Cleveland Cavaliers were not yet a reality (they began play in 1970), but who would have believed this franchise would reach the Eastern Conference finals only three times in its history, and into the NBA Championship series only once (in the franchise's 37th year)? As for hockey, Cleveland was unable to sustain even its membership in the NHL, much less entertain Stanley Cup dreams.

Forty-three years is a long time. And that's not even the whole story. The Cleveland Indians last captured a World Series title in 1948, although they at least have made it to the Series three times since then. The Browns last won it all in 1964, but came tantalizingly close numerous times. They have yet to be one of the hyped teams who went to a Super Bowl. The Cavs, well, except for 2007, they haven't really come close. In the many Cleveland sports seasons that have come and gone, not only have championships been non-existent, but heartbreak has been a steady reality for so many.

Two stories capture the impetus behind this book. The first story relates to my years as a college student at Miami University in the late 1980s and early 1990s. It was a heady time in Cleveland sports, as the Cavs and Browns were competitive in those years, and I soon became known in my fraternity as one of the diehard Cleveland fans, inspiring ridicule as I watched Cleveland sports teams in action. One friend, a Toledo native, used to goad me into a conversation about Cleveland sports teams with a dialogue that would begin, "So the _____ (fill in your preferred Cleveland sports team here) are going to be pretty good this year, don't you think?"

Naively grabbing the bait, I would excitedly rattle off the players and facts that made his question seem like a statement. My blood pressure and excitement level would rise as I continued to spew my dribble. Midway through my commentary, he would shake his head, laugh, and walk away, saying "Hook, line, and sinker, every time."

After walking into this routine more than a dozen times as if it were Abbott and Costello's practiced "Who's on first?" routine, I finally asked what his deal was.

His response: "I will be dead before Cleveland wins a championship in any major sport."

What a slap in the face from a Toledo native whose favorite teams were the great teams from the 1970s (the Boston Celtics, Pittsburgh Steelers, and Cincinnati Reds). As a kid, he chose his teams after they each had won their championships, and in college he would say, "Well, at least I'm still loyal to them." Yeah, tough to be a loyal fan of those teams, who have racked up championships like a hunter does deer heads. A guy from Toledo, whose most legendary team is the Mudhens, for Pete's sake, was giving me hell.

Fast forward to September 1995, when the Cleveland Indians set baseball records and then captured its first American League pennant in 41 years. I found a sympathy card in the store and sent it to him, writing that I understood he must be on his deathbed, what with the Cleveland Indians four games away from winning it all. I sent my sympathies to him and his family, and promised to attend the funeral just after the Indians were done taking care of the Atlanta Braves.

What a maroon I was.

Six games and one Atlanta Braves World Series Championship later, I received a card in the mail from my Toledo friend. In the card were taped three items: a hook, a line, and a sinker; with only the words "Every time" at the bottom.

Yep.

The second story has its origins in the strike-shortened major league baseball season of 1994. The early August end to the season soured me, as it was beyond my comprehension that, in the whole cosmic scheme of things, some Greater Power could allow the stoppage of a season in which the Tribe was one measly game out of first place in the American League Central Division. (Admittedly, at this time I probably could have benefited from a re-evaluation of my own spiritual beliefs.)

Having been born in 1970, I had no comprehension that teams could be anywhere within 23 games of the first-place team in August. So there I was, this desperate fan whose favorite team was snatched away in the face of impending glory. Perhaps I should be happy - the long history of Cleveland sports teams over the last decades suggests that the end of the 1994 season probably would have ended with a crushing disappointment.

prologue

The strike made it hard for me to fall in love with the 1995 Indians, what with the rumors in the national media during spring training that the season might not happen or might be shortened. Anyway, the 1995 season and pennant and trip to the World Series was amazing. But I have to admit I didn't even know how to act during the World Series - I felt like it was my first car date and I didn't know what to do or say, and I was probably babbling incessantly as I did as a 16-year-old about fascinating topics like the Stray Cats or the A-Team or something stupid like that. Picture Ben Stiller in *Something About Mary*.

Anyway, just over a week after the Indians' loss in the Series, Art Modell took the rostrum in downtown Baltimore and announced the move of the Cleveland Browns to Baltimore.

I sat dumbfounded listening to the radio news. I decided I couldn't take any more. Perhaps I would just become a fan of high school sports - you know, the players are just kids, they are hungrier for it, it's not just a business to them, blah, blah, blah. After all, my alma mater, St. Ignatius, had actually captured national football championships. That was it . . . I would just be a fan of high school sports. I was so offended by the owners' casual disregard for the fans that I swore off professional sports for good.

I decided never again would I throw myself behind a professional team. And I really tried. I did everything I could not to get excited by the amazing Indians' runs in the late 1990s. I attempted to squelch my enthusiasm when the Browns took the field in Canton amid the hoopla of the return of professional football to Cleveland. I told myself that chapter of my life was over. As the years went on, of course, my decision was an easy one, I recognize now. The Browns were horrible for their first few years back in the NFL, and the Cavs were just, well, boring. The Indians made it tough for me to keep my opposition to professional sports, but of course after the run in the 1990s they started to fall from the playoffs every autumn just like the leaves did from the trees, so walking past the TV was not that difficult.

Then, the 2002 Browns' season began. Sunday after Sunday, I told myself I didn't care. I was done with professional sports. My heart tugged at me, though. I guess I discovered some inner voices. At first I was troubled by the voices. But then I started to listen to them. First they said, "Remember the Kardiac Kids. Remember Brian Sipe. Remember the double-overtime playoff win against the Jets." And then soon after that, the voices chimed in with . . . "Remember the Drive." That's right, I would remind myself. "Remember the damn Drive, Fumble, Modell's announcement, Red Right 88, Game 7." No more.

I wrestled internally. And then the Browns made it to the playoffs. The pull was too strong. Like Darth Vader to the dark side of the Force, I couldn't resist. I woke up that day and decided I would put on my Cleveland Browns' t-shirt and hat. Just this one time I'd show my civic pride. That's all it was. I would watch the game by myself so I could deal in my own special way. It couldn't hurt - what the heck, I didn't have any expectations, right?

Then they did it. Abusing the Steelers as if they wanted the Super Bowl, the Browns racked up an impressive first half that was so lopsided, I almost started to blush for the Yinzers in Steeltown. Then, into the room strolled my wife, a Pittsburgh native and Steelers' fan. (I blush to acknowledge it.)

But wait, I told myself. Wait.

As the clock ticked off the seconds

ending the third quarter, Browns quarterback (and at that moment during the game, all-pro, Canton-bound) Kelly Holcomb lead the team downfield and on a third-and-one at the Steelers' six-yard line, he was flushed out of the pocket and, instead of running, tried to get the ball to Jamel White. It fell incomplete, and the Browns settled for a field goal to go ahead, 27-14. At that moment, I turned to my wife and said, "That's it. They just lost it. They just allowed the Steelers back into the game."

"What a freak," my wife said. "How ridiculous. Look at the score."

I responded, with a "You watch — the Browns will fall apart." Then I added, "You just don't know what it's like. You just have no idea what it's like to be a Cleveland fan."

Final score: Pittsburgh 36, Cleveland 33. And the calls from my Pittsburgh relatives just added a bit of salt to that already gaping "I'm-a-Cleveland-sports-fan" wound I've been sporting for 37 years.

I wrote this book to capture what it's been like to be a Cleveland sports fan over the last four-plus decades. Outsiders don't know. Only insiders get it. We're a proud, fierce, desperate bunch, and we tell ourselves that if there were some sort of championship for fans, we'd win that. We tell ourselves that, of course, because since 1964 we haven't had the chance to partake in any NBA title, World Series victory, or Super Bowl championship.

But that doesn't stop us from yearning, hoping, yelling, praying, and, ultimately, coming back to the Browns, Indians, and Cavaliers.

They get us, every time.

Hook, line, and sinker.

Pittsburgh quarterback Tommy Maddox celebrates after throwing the game-winning touchdown in the fourth quarter of the 2002 playoff matchup between the two archrivals, capping a comeback win for the Steelers and a heartbreaking loss for the Browns. *(David Richard photo)*

bragging rights
surviving the drought

We have not journeyed all this way across the centuries, across the oceans, across the mountains, across the prairies, because we're made of sugar candy. — Winston Churchill

We humans seem to have a proclivity for one-upmanship. If someone tells us that he or she just got a great deal on a new home entertainment center - zero down and no payments for six months - it feels good to be able to say, "That's great, but we also got zero interest and no payments for a whole year." The rules of conversation, however, make it clear that too often coming out better than our friends is risky. Modesty is more appealing.

A safer approach to the one-upmanship game centers on human misery. It is much more acceptable to have screwed up worse than our buddy. "Man, I had an awful ride into work this morning. I-90 was like a parking lot, and I got into work 15 minutes late." To which it is safe to reply: "Tell me about it! I was stuck in it too, so I had the bright idea to go over to the Shoreway. Dumb! A broken-down truck on the Main Avenue Bridge got me to work a half hour late." For some reason, to one-up another with worse luck is almost endearing.

Sports, of course, is a major topic for discussion, and it abounds in opportunities for comparisons. A Cleveland sports fan cannot help but lament his city's championship drought. But can he make the case to his co-sufferers across the fruited plain that he has had a more frustrating time of it than they have? Sports writer Jack McCallum would seem to agree. In *Sports Illustrated*, he says that "Cleveland is the city of true sports misery." Probably most Clevelanders think he has it right.

Of course, misery and pain are subjective. How can anyone know if his or her sprained ankle hurts more than someone else's? It is probably impossible to know for sure that Cleveland fans are the most frustrated among those in the 48 major

surviving the drought: cleveland sports fans since 1964

Fans line the perimeter of Fleming Field as the Browns practice for their 1965 NFL championship game against the Green Bay Packers. The Packers won the big game 23-12. It was the last time the Browns made it to the final game.
(Norbert Yassanye photo, Cleveland Public Library collection)

league cities. But, that proviso aside, we Clevelanders can make a pretty good objective case about the depth of our sports woes, and in light of that to claim for ourselves the title of "most faithful," or the "most resilient," if not the "best" that can be found in any major league city. Cleveland fans are truly a special breed.

So let's try to prove our case. When we say a "major league" city, we think we are on safe grounds to include only those cities which have a franchise in baseball, football, basketball, or hockey. Polo, lacrosse, and soccer just do not cut it. It is also relatively inarguable to identify the "major" leagues from the "minors." The major leagues of the four most important sports are composed of 122 franchises. These are spread out across 48 "major league" cities, 43 in the U.S. and five more in Canada, our neighbor to the north. The franchise list looks like this:

Major League Baseball (MLB)	30 teams
National Football League (NFL)	32 teams
National Basketball Assoc. (NBA)	30 teams
National Hockey League (NHL)	30 teams

We suppose that some might want to argue that certain cities are more "major league" than others. After all, New York City is home to quite a few franchises whereas Salt Lake City has only one. But for our purposes, we have considered a city "major league" even if it is home to only one big league team.

Identifying the number of these major league cities takes more than a quick glance at the newspaper standings. For example, some franchises are named after states instead of cities. The Colorado Rockies and the Denver Nuggets are one example. They both play in Denver. The

chapter 1: bragging rights

Cleveland fans have always come in droves to the lakefront to watch the Indians and Browns. In the 1950s and 1960s, they could see some amazing players and teams, even when victories were scarce.
(Charles Proctor photo, Western Reserve Historical Society)

Golden State Warriors play in Oakland. Then there are the Texas Rangers and the Dallas Cowboys. The Rangers play in Arlington, Texas, midway between Fort Worth and Dallas, about 15 miles from both. We think the case is solid that the Rangers can be "assigned" to Dallas.

While we accept that Anaheim is distinct from Los Angeles and for some time called its team the California Angels, Anaheim exists within the map's colored sprawl of the larger city. That reality prompted the team in 2006 to rename itself as the Los Angeles Angels of Anaheim.

Minnesota is the chosen name for the three franchises that play in Minneapolis and the one that plays in St. Paul. But, what the heck, these are known as the "twin cities," so we will treat the two as one.

On the other hand, Carolina sports two teams, but the NFL Panthers play in Charlotte, while the NHL Hurricanes play in Raleigh. Tennessee has three teams, but only one is named for the state; the NFL's Tennessee Titans play in Nashville, located in the middle of the state. The NHL team also plays there, but it is known as the Nashville (not Tennessee) Predators. The other Tennessee team, the NBA Grizzlies, is named after its host city of Memphis, situated at the state's western border.

How about the NFL Giants and Jets? They both play in East Rutherford, New Jersey, but for some reason are known as the New York Giants and the New York Jets. The basketball and hockey teams that play in East Rutherford are called respectively the New Jersey Nets and the New Jersey Devils. East Rutherford, New Jersey, however, is just across the Hudson River from Manhattan, and closer to the Big Apple than Richfield is to Cleveland. The Cavaliers were the Cleveland Cavaliers when they played in Richfield,

surviving the drought: cleveland sports fans since 1964

Third baseman Toby Harrah swings for the fence. Though Harrah only played for the Indians for five seasons - and bleak seasons they were - in 2001 he was voted by the fans as one of the favorite Indians of all time. Note the number of fans in the stands. *(Janet Macoska photo, Western Reserve Historical Society)*

and so on similar grounds we think that it is not unreasonable to assign the Nets and Devils to New York City. No offense to New Jersey intended. Honest. The NHL Florida Panthers play in Sunrise, Florida, about equidistant from Fort Lauderdale and Miami, but we feel safe it assigning that team to Miami where it was originally rooted.

The place names for the teams actually seem to have more to do with political and marketing concerns than with actual geographic considerations. Some play in urban centers; others are located in the suburbs or farther out into the exurbs (e.g. Foxboro, Massachusetts). We have assigned the teams to the principal cities that define the metropolitan area.

Our rules for assigning locations were as follows:

1) If the franchise bore a city's name, we assigned it to that city;

2) If a franchise bore a state's or region's name, we assigned it to the city or region (e.g. Twin Cities or Tampa Bay) in which it played;

3) If a franchise bore a state's name, but played within the confines of a U.S. Census Bureau statistical area, we assigned it to the major city in that metropolitan zone.

So now that we have explained the tortuous thinking that illustrates our method for assigning certain teams to certain cities, we can proceed with our list.

Three cities have more than four franchises. Ten have four. Another eight have three franchises. Eleven have two. And 16 cities are home to a single franchise.

The following tables give the breakdown. The first table lists those "super" major league cities, those with four or more franchises.

chapter 1: bragging rights

MAJOR LEAGUE CITIES WITH FOUR OR MORE FRANCHISES		
CITY	NUMBER OF TEAMS	TEAM NAMES
New York City	9	Mets, Yankees, Giants, Jets, Knicks, Islanders, Rangers, New Jersey Nets, New Jersey Devils
Los Angeles	6	Dodgers, Angels, Lakers, Clippers, Kings, Mighty Ducks
Chicago	5	Cubs, White Sox, Bears, Bulls, Blackhawks
Atlanta	4	Braves, Falcons, Hawks, Thrashers
Boston	4	Red Sox, New England Patriots, Celtics, Bruins
Dallas	4	Texas Rangers, Cowboys, Mavericks, Stars
Denver	4	Colorado Rockies, Broncos, Nuggets, Colorado Avalanche
Detroit	4	Tigers, Lions, Pistons, Red Wings
Miami	4	Florida Marlins, Dolphins, Heat, Florida Panthers
Minneapolis-St.Paul	4	Twins, Vikings, Timberwolves, Wild
Philadelphia	4	Phillies, Eagles, 76ers, Flyers
Phoenix	4	Arizona Diamondbacks, Arizona Cardinals, Suns, Coyotes
Washington, D.C.	4	Nationals, Redskins, Wizards, Capitals

Note: Los Angeles is the only city on this list which is not home to all four major sports (it lost its football franchise to St. Louis).

MAJOR LEAGUE CITIES WITH THREE FRANCHISES		
CITY	NUMBER OF TEAMS	TEAM NAMES
Cleveland	**3**	**Indians, Browns, Cavaliers**
Houston	3	Astros, Rockets, Texans
Oakland	3	A's, Raiders, Golden State Warriors
Pittsburgh	3	Pirates, Steelers, Penguins
St. Louis	3	Cardinals, Rams, Blues
Seattle	3	Mariners, Seahawks, SuperSonics
Tampa Bay Tampa/St. Petersburg	3	Devil Rays, Buccaneers, Lightning
Toronto	3	Blue Jays, Raptors, Maple Leafs

surviving the drought: cleveland sports fans since 1964

MAJOR LEAGUE CITIES WITH TWO FRANCHISES		
CITY	NUMBER OF TEAMS	TEAM NAMES
Baltimore	2	Orioles, Ravens
Buffalo	2	Bills, Sabres
Charlotte	2	Carolina Panthers, Bobcats
Cincinnati	2	Reds, Bengals
Indianapolis	2	Colts, Indiana Pacers
Kansas City	2	Royals, Chiefs
Milwaukee	2	Brewers, Bucks
Nashville	2	Tennessee Titans, Predators
New Orleans	2	Saints, Hornets
San Diego	2	Padres, Chargers
San Francisco	2	Giants, 49ers

MAJOR LEAGUE CITIES WITH ONE FRANCHISE		
CITY	NUMBER OF TEAMS	TEAM NAMES
Calgary	1	Flames
Columbus	1	Blue Jackets
Edmonton	1	Oilers
Green Bay	1	Packers
Jacksonville	1	Jaguars
Memphis	1	Grizzlies
Montreal	1	Canadiens
Orlando	1	Magic
Ottawa	1	Senators
Portland	1	Trailblazers
Raleigh	1	Carolina Hurricanes
Sacramento	1	Kings
Salt Lake City	1	Utah Jazz
San Antonio	1	Spurs
San Jose	1	Sharks
Vancouver	1	Canucks

chapter 1: bragging rights

During the 1970s, the Indians never finished higher that fourth place and had only two winning seasons. Gaylord Perry, however, twice won more than 20 games, leading some opponents to suspect that he was doctoring the ball. Here he passes inspection. *(Cleveland Indians photo, Cleveland Landmarks Press collection)*

The thesis of this book is that Cleveland sports fans are a special breed, and that they have earned the right to win the one-upmanship argument about sports misery. Naturally, that does not prohibit supporters of other frustrated cities from making their claims. Bring them on.

In October 2003 national attention was riveted on the Chicago Cubs and the Boston Red Sox who had made it to the baseball playoffs. Both teams became sentimental favorites, because it had been a very long time since either of them had won a World Series. Most fans thought it would be pretty cool if these two could face each other in the fall classic. But once again, after tantalizing their cheering fans, they fell short, each succumbing to their opponents in the seventh game of the league championship series.

Indeed, most series watchers probably felt the pain of Red Sox fans as their team was once again denied. Bostonians, after all, had been lamenting the fate of their Red Sox for a long time. The team had not won a World Series since 1918. We do not wish to deny the frustration that the long-suffering baseball fans in that city had experienced - until the World Series drought finally ended in 2004 when the Red Sox defeated the St. Louis Cardinals in four straight games. But even before the euphoria that came with the 2004 crown settled in, Boston fans had experienced plenty to cheer about; their other major league teams had given the city a multitude of championships to celebrate. Caught up in the hype, casual observers easily glossed over the city's other major sport triumphs, 15 of them in the last 42 years.

But Cleveland fans are anything but casual, and so it was inevitable for them to point out: Quit whining, Boston. Your

surviving the drought: cleveland sports fans since 1964

When it rains, it pours. Only in Cleveland Municipal Stadium, the rain was not simply cause for delaying the game - for the Minnesota Twins, it meant finding the high ground in two feet of water. *(Ron Kuntz photo)*

complaining, despite the nine Celtics titles since 1964 - the last being in 1986 - and the three Patriots titles since 2001, bores us.

And how about those poor Chicago Cubs? They haven't won a World Series since 1908. There are few, if any, Cub fans still alive who can remember that distant triumph. But like Boston, Chicago has crossed the finish line a winner eight times with its other franchises. Two years later came the saga of the Cubs' cross-town baseball team. The White Sox had not one a World Series since 1917, and then in 1919 there came the Black Sox scandal. Had that scandal cursed the franchise ever since? This was how the media played it up as the White Sox faced the Houston Astros in the 2005 World Series. Four games later, the White Sox were world champs. End of the curse. The Cubs may still be hoping for their day in the sun, but Chicago fans, unlike those from Cleveland, have had much to celebrate in the last four-plus decades.

In fact, every one of the "super" major league cities, those with four or more franchises, has experienced the winner's circle since 1964. Their crowns number as follows (data are current through the 2006-2007 seasons for the National Hockey League and the National Basketball Association):

The next time a Cleveland sports team wins a championship, I will . . .

"rise up from my grave and get a one-day pass to Hell so I can taunt Art Modell," — John Summers, Mentor

chapter 1: bragging rights

Browns' fans, regardless of their age, know of the awesome record their team compiled between 1946 and 1962 under founding head coach Paul Brown. During those years they compiled victories at a .707 clip. Most fans pine for a return to that glory. *(Cleveland Browns photo, Cleveland Landmarks Press collection)*

surviving the drought: cleveland sports fans since 1964

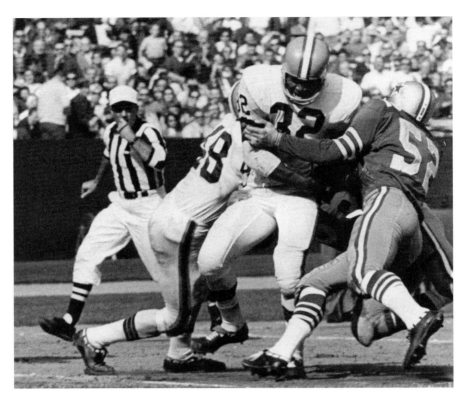

Jim Brown was the greatest running back the Browns ever had. He was part of the glory years, retiring in 1965 with 12,312 rushing yards and 126 touchdowns to his credit.
(Robert Quinlan photo, Cleveland Public Library collection)

CHAMPIONSHIPS WON: 1965-2007 FOUR – OR MORE – FRANCHISE CITIES	
New York City	21
Los Angeles	15
Boston	12
Detroit	9
Chicago	8
Dallas	6
Philadelphia	5
Miami	5
Washington, DC	4
Denver	2
Minnesota	2
Atlanta	1
Phoenix	1

While probably not in the tradition of great sportsmanship, Clevelanders can be permitted to at least be rankled by Atlanta's single triumph. The Atlanta Braves made it to post-season play every year from 1995, the year the current playoff system came into effect, to 2005. And year after year they have been eliminated before claiming the final prize. Except, that is, in 1995 when Atlanta beat Cleveland, then experiencing its first fling at the World Series since 1954. Atlanta fans had a sweet victory to savor. Cleveland fans continued suffering through their drought.

New York's 21 titles are ample explanation for Clevelanders' strong antipathy for that city's teams (really though, the hostility is directed only at the baseball Yankees, who have accounted for eight of those season crowns).

Cleveland is one of eight cities with three major league franchises. Briefly we had four. The NHL Cleveland Barons were with us for just two seasons, 1976-1977 and 1977-1978. Those were miserable winters on the North Coast, and

chapter 1: bragging rights

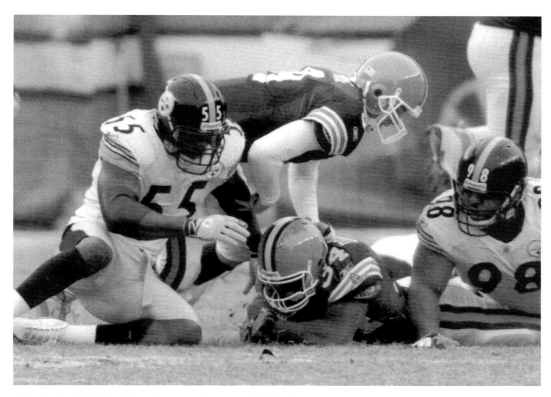

Running back Reuben Droughns struggles to regain the ball after a fumbled handoff during a 2006 game against the Pittsburgh Steelers. Since the return of the Browns in 1999, sadly this has been standard. Quarterback Charley Frye is in the background. *(Ron Kuntz photo)*

the team was playing in the accessibility-challenged Richfield Coliseum. Poor play and terrible weather resulted in too few fans in the seats. At the end of the second season, the Barons were merged into the Minnesota North Stars. A cash-strapped franchise which won only 47 games in two years during the region's worst back-to-back winters was hardly a true test of the city's support for hockey. Nonetheless, the Baron's departure was a blow to the city's prestige, ending its brief stay on the "super big league city" list. Maybe someday, Cleveland will have another shot at the NHL. But that is another story.

So how does Cleveland compare with our current three-franchise peer group? As the following list shows, every city but one has gone the distance. That one? Cleveland.

CHAMPIONSHIPS WON: 1965-2007 THREE-FRANCHISE CITIES	
Pittsburgh	9
Oakland	7
St. Louis	5
Toronto	4
Houston	2
Tampa Bay	2
Seattle	1
Cleveland	**0**

There are two features to this list that gall Clevelanders. First of all, there is arch-rival Pittsburgh at the top. Painful enough.

Less obvious perhaps is the Tampa Bay entry. Like Clevelanders, until January 2003 Tampa Bay fans had not tasted the top prize, but then fortune smiled on them when they won Super Bowl XXXVII.

surviving the drought: cleveland sports fans since 1964

Art Modell owned the Cleveland Browns for 35 years, but in that tenure the team never made it to the Super Bowl. Then he moved the franchise to Baltimore where his newly named Ravens won the crown in just six years. Just one more reason for Browns' fans to feel the pain. *(Cleveland* Press *Collection of the Cleveland State University Libraries)*

A comparison of the two franchises helps illustrate just how pathetic Cleveland's zero is.

Beginning in 1965, Cleveland has had 41 chances to win a World Series (no Series in 1994), 39 chances to win either the NFL Crown or the Super Bowl (there was the franchise hiatus of 1996-1998), and 37 chances for the Cavaliers to snare an NBA championship. So Cleveland fans have gone 0 for 117 tries. That is a record of futility that fans in no other city have to bear.

Tampa Bay, on the other hand, is relatively new to the major league circle. Tampa Bay's NFL Buccaneers date from 1976, its NHL Lightning from 1992, and its baseball Devil Rays from 1998. Florida's West Coast teams failed in their quest for the top prize only 44 times. Then they took the gold, winning the Super Bowl in 2003 and the Stanley Cup in 2004. Tampa Bay made it to the championship rank in considerably fewer than half the attempts that Cleveland teams have aspired to a title.

Looking at the franchises in the 11 two-team and 16 one-team cities, we can find quite a few more teams that have never won a major championship. On the other hand, quite a few have, all with fewer chances than Cleveland has had.

The next time a Cleveland sports team wins a championship, I will . . .

"make sure my son and I go to celebrate,"

— Frank Oley, Mayfield Heights

chapter 1: bragging rights

For many seasons baseball fans in Cleveland had little to cheer. Frequently promotions provided the chief entertainment at Cleveland Municipal Stadium. Here the San Diego Chicken, joined by four Indians pitchers, entertains the crowd with an air-guitar concert. *(Janet Macoska photo, Western Reserve Historical Society collection)*

There have been 12 winners in these two categories, combining for a total of 45 titles:

CHAMPIONSHIPS WON: 1965-2007 ONE- AND TWO-FRANCHISE CITIES	
Montreal	12
Edmonton	6
Green Bay	5
Baltimore	5
San Francisco	5
San Antonio	4
Cincinnati	3
Kansas City	2
Buffalo	1
Calgary	1
Indianapolis	1
Milwaukee	1
Portland	1
Raleigh	1

Buffalo's victory stems from 1965 when it won the American Football League championship. The Super Bowl began following the 1966 seasons of the AFL and NFL. Since the AFL records have been accepted into the NFL on equal footing, Buffalo's win counts as a major championship in the same way the Cleveland's 1964 NFL win does.

A total of 34 of the 48 major league cities have won at least one championship since 1964. That leaves 14 teams, all from the one- or two-team lists, who have been winless in that same time frame.

surviving the drought: cleveland sports fans since 1964

Bobby "Bingo" Smith is probably the best remembered player from the inaugural Cavaliers basketball squad during the 1970-1971 season. The 6'5" forward spent a decade with the team, and was a sure hand at the foul line.
(Cleveland Press Collection of the Cleveland State University Libraries)

CITIES WITHOUT CHAMPIONSHIPS WON: 1965-2007
Charlotte
Cleveland
Columbus
Jacksonville
Memphis
Nashville
New Orleans
Orlando
Ottawa
Sacramento
Salt Lake City
San Diego
San Jose
Vancouver

Even a quick glance at this list of "losers" reveals that all of these - except Cleveland - are "expansion" franchises. "Expansion," though, does not necessarily mean recent.

The American Football League (AFL) came into existence in 1960, and it was not fully absorbed into the NFL until 1970. San Diego earned a spot in 1961 when it relocated from Los Angeles. The San Diego Chargers won the AFL title in 1963. The Padres' baseball franchise was awarded in 1969, and it has not yet won. So technically the fans of San Diego have faced a championship drought one year longer than Clevelanders have. Clevelanders can no doubt also sympathize with San Diego fans' disappointment when their teams came close; the Chargers lost in their only Super Bowl appearance in 1995, and then lost in the NFL Conference semi-finals in 2007; the Padres were eliminated in the 2006 baseball playoffs. But while the San Diego drought may be longer, it is not deeper. Since San Diego has only two franchises, it has gone 0 for 81 in championship tries, clearly a frustrating history. Cleveland's 0 for 117 record,

chapter 1: bragging rights

In 1976 Cavs' coach Bill Fitch brought his team back to the Cleveland Arena for a last visit before the building was demolished. The Cavs played at the diminutive facility their first four seasons as they awaited completion of their new home in Richfield. *(Cleveland* Press *Collection of the Cleveland State University Libraries)*

however, easily tops that and leaves Clevelanders the most thwarted among the fans in all 48 major league cities. The following table of non-winners makes the point clear.

CITY	UNSUCCESSFUL QUESTS
Cleveland	**117**
San Diego	81
New Orleans	58
Vancouver	37
Salt Lake City	33
Sacramento	22
Orlando	18
San Jose	16
Ottawa	15
Charlotte	15
Jacksonville	12
Memphis	12
Nashville	10
Columbus	7

Compared to all the other major league cities, Cleveland is clearly suffering a most distressing championship funk, and its sports fans have obviously earned bragging rights about being the most frustrated of those in any major league city.

That is not to say that Cleveland teams have been consistently inept, although some editions of them have been. A closer look at each of Cleveland's three major league franchises will provide a further look at the reasons behind the levels of disappointment that Cleveland fans have faced.

Historically, the Cleveland Browns were the city's most dominating team, and they brought much rejoicing to the city in its early years, but 1964, 43 years ago, was their last league championship. There have been some exciting seasons (who can forget the Kardiac Kids?) since then, resulting in 15 playoff appearances, but since that

Although the turf in old Municipal Stadium was rarely in pristine condition, it didn't deter fans. Here, a full crowd took in one of the last Tribe games at the end of the 1993 season, before the team moved to its new home at Ontario and East Ninth streets. *(Cleveland Stadium Corporation photo, Cleveland Landmarks Press)*

championship year the team has had as many losing as winning season records, 18 of each (along with three .500 seasons).

Their overall win-loss record from 1946 through 1995 was 374-266 (not counting ties), for a .584 winning percentage. But if the Browns' win-loss percentage only covers 1965-2006, then it drops to .485.

Cleveland and its sports fans suffered a grievous loss at the end of the 1995 season, when Art Modell moved the franchise to Baltimore. The outrage of Cleveland supporters was so loud and their clamor so dynamic and so ardent that the NFL promised the city a reborn Browns team in 1999. The fans eagerly awaited the team's reappearance. They watched the razing of old Cleveland Municipal Stadium and the rising of the new Cleveland Browns Stadium. And they dreamt of the city's return to its historic football glory. Yet, after eight seasons, the "new" Browns have crafted a feeble 40-88 won-loss record, a .312 winning percentage - a far cry from the fabled days of Paul Brown.

Browns' fans have been urged to be patient, and they have remained loyal and hopeful. But they must wonder just why it is that the new Browns have managed such little success when compared with the Carolina Panthers and Jacksonville Jaguars who began play during the "old" Browns' final season in 1995. In its first eight years Carolina went 53-75, and while not an impressive record, they sported a winning percentage one hundred points better than that of the Browns. Carolina also made a trip to the Super Bowl in 2004. Jacksonville has also done considerably better than the "new" Browns, crafting a 67-61 record in its first eight years, for a .523 winning percentage.

Even more galling for Browns' fans was the 2000 Super Bowl victory for the

chapter 1: bragging rights

Lebron James will not be denied as he goes in for a lay-up. In James the Cavaliers found the superstar who would take the team from a 17-65 season to the Finals in only a few years. *(Karin McKenna photo)*

Baltimore Ravens, the "old" Browns. After decades of failure in Cleveland, Art Modell's team won the Super Bowl in just its fifth year in its new Baltimore home. Cleveland fans could only wonder why.

Since the Super Bowl's 1967 inception, 27 of the 32 NFL teams have made the trip to the big game. Cleveland is one of five who remain on the waiting list, along with Phoenix (Arizona), Detroit, Jacksonville, and New Orleans. Cleveland Browns' fans keep the faith, but they have to wonder what evil spell keeps the wind from billowing their sails.

The Cleveland Indians baseball team, the city's oldest sports franchise, has played at a .485 clip since 1964, a record more mediocre than miserable (although the four times it lost more than 100 games, in 1971, 1985, 1987, and 1991, it clearly was miserable). Overall, during this stretch the team has managed only 13 winning seasons, while chalking up 29 losing ones. Even worse, they have not won a World Series since 1948, a record of woe only exceeded by that of the Chicago Cubs. Yet in that stretch there were also six first-place and two second-place division finishes, and two trips to the World Series (in 1995 and 1997). An interesting question about frustration arises. What is more frustrating, to lose 105 games, or to lose the seventh game of the World Series? But more on that later.

And then there are the Cleveland Cavaliers. Cleveland's basketball franchise was launched for the 1970-1971 season, and therefore it has not been able to frustrate its hometown fans for as long as the Browns or the Indians. Their win-loss percentage stands at .449, giving the Cavs the dubious distinction of having had less success than either the Browns or the Indians. In the team's 37-year history, it

surviving the drought: cleveland sports fans since 1964

Bill Fitch was the Cavs' first coach. He led the team for nine seasons, the longest tenure at the team's helm, presided over the "miracle" season, and more commonly cheered on his often struggling players.
(Cleveland Press *Collection of the Cleveland State University Libraries)*

has provided some thrills, memorably the 1975-1976 "Miracle of Richfield" season when they made it all the way to the Eastern Conference finals, before succumbing there to the Boston Celtics, 4-2. They got that close again in 1991-1992, before the Chicago Bulls claimed conference honors, 4-2. Then came a series of so-so or not even so-so years. In 2002-2003 the team was 17-65.

Cavs' fans, however, found a new reason for hope just before the 2003-2004 season, when Northern Ohio high school basketball phenom LeBron James became the team's first-round draft pick. The outlook for the team suddenly became much brighter. In LeBron's first year, the team more than doubled its previous year record, going to 35-47. The following year, the Cavs put together a winning season,

The next time a Cleveland sports team wins a championship, I will . . .
"be in the happy hunting ground," — Don Friedt, Akron

chapter 1: bragging rights

The energy Cleveland fans bring to their home teams can be amazing. During the 2006-2007 Cavaliers fans were frequently on their feet as the electronic message urges. There was plenty to cheer about as the team brought their long-waiting fans the franchise's first Eastern Conference championship. *(Karin McKenna photo)*

42-40, and while the team did not make the playoffs, hope among the long-suffering fans began to grow.

In 2005-2006 hope grew brighter. The team put together a 50-32 record and made it to the playoffs for the 14th time in its history. The team made it to the second round before losing to the Detroit Pistons in seven games. Fans began to think about "next year."

The "next year," 2006-2007, was even better. Achieving another 50-32 regular season record, the Cavs again made the playoffs. They put away the Washington Wizards and then the New Jersey Nets. Then came the Pistons, who had ended their run a year earlier, and the chance to win the Eastern Conference crown. Detroit won the first two games in the series, and only twice before in NBA history did a team which was down 0-2 ever overcome that deficit. But the Cavs did it. They won the third and fourth games at home, and then in Detroit, behind the brilliant play of LeBron James - who scored 48 points - they won the fifth game in double overtime. The sixth game was back in Cleveland, and for three quarters it was tight. In the fourth quarter, however, rookie Daniel "Boobie" Gibson reeled off five three-point plays, and the Cavs won the Eastern Conference Championship for the first time in their 37-year history. The game was witnessed by a capacity crowd at the Q, and thousands more watched on jumbo screens set up in the Gateway Plaza. The cheering and the fireworks went on well into the night. The NBA

surviving the drought: cleveland sports fans since 1964

LeBron James and the rest of the 2006-7 Cavaliers came closer than any other Cavs team in history to the trophy and an NBA championship. *(David Richard photo)*

finals, against Western Conference champs San Antonio Spurs, awaited.

Although the experts had predicted a Spurs' victory (they had won three championships in the previous eight years), Cleveland fans were buoyed by the exciting play their team had shown during the first three rounds of the playoffs. Clevelanders were also glad at the media coverage of their city and the recognition given to its sports miseries over the previous decades. But in the end, the experts were right. The Spurs won the series, 4-0, forcing Cleveland fans once again to think in terms of "next year." The consolation was that the Cavs were a young team which had been showing steady improvement, and its star LeBron James was only 22 years old. Yet, once again ultimate victory had been denied. It hurt.

So these are the bare facts involved in Cleveland's long professional sports famine, a dry spell that has, however, neither dulled Cleveland fans' capacity for hope nor its appetite for victory. Clevelanders are a resilient bunch. Living on the North Shore makes that inevitable.

The statistics establish that Cleveland fans have every right to play the one-up-man-ship game of woe and lamentation, and that is not all bad. The misery does help us to bond. But statistics, however central they are to the fabric of sports, only provide the story's skeleton. They cannot and do not reveal the myriad ways in which Cleveland fans have experienced frustration over the past 43 years. There have been some real zingers. Let's take a look at some of them. It will add muscle to our bragging rights and help us bond even more.

heartbreak
surviving the drought

Victory belongs to the most persevering. — Napoleon Bonaparte

To outsiders, Cleveland sports go from one heartbreaking moment to the next. Come to think of it, to Clevelanders, Cleveland sports go from one heartbreaking moment to the next.

Actually, it's not true. Cleveland's championship-less existence in the last 43 years has from time to time given fans a break from total misery. It would be more accurate to say that as of late, the Cleveland sports scene has largely witnessed poor or mediocre teams, punctuated by a team every once in a long while that gives us hope for a brief moment before retreating back to mediocrity and tearing out our hearts and assaulting our sanity.

In these decades of emotional challenge, robbing Cleveland sports fans of any vestige of emotional equilibrium probably began with the rise of the Kardiac Kids in 1980. By the time the brown and orange strapped on their cleats in August 1980, Cleveland sports had just finished an awful decade. The Cavaliers, who entered the NBA as an expansion franchise, began its first season in 1970 with a total of 15 wins and ended the decade with a 37-45 record, capping a ten-year span in which they sported a miserable .416 winning percentage (341-479) and one glorious trip to the playoffs. The Indians in 1970 ended their season 76-86 and in fifth place in the American League East. For the rest of the decade, they would never reach higher than fourth place in the division (1974-76), and ended the 70s show with a .488 overall winning percentage (737-774).

For the Browns, the 1970s was a fall from grace. The franchise had dominated professional football from the mid-1940s through the 1950s, and by the time the 1960s came around, they continued their

surviving the drought: cleveland sports fans since 1964

Center Jim Chones uses his 6'11" to advantage as he dunks the ball. Chones played with the Cavs from 1974 through 1979, and was a key part of the "Miracle of Richfield" squad in 1976.
(Cleveland Press *Collection of the Cleveland State University Libraries)*

annual trips to the playoffs. Although they had won their last championship in 1964, they continued to make the playoffs through 1969. When 1970 began, the Browns finished 7-7, and the team would end the decade with a marginal .500 winning percentage (72-70-2).

So, when the 1980 Browns took the field, they began to create excitement in Cleveland not seen in years. Partially what made the 1980 season so special came from the fact that during the 1970s bad news seemed to be around virtually every corner for Clevelanders. When the 1980 team gave the fans exciting games and 11 victories, it became easier to forget about the city's default on loans, or the Hough and Glenville riots, or the Cuyahoga River catching on fire. In fact, those seemed like distant memories when Brian Sipe and company leaped from their Municipal Stadium dugout onto the turf.

The next time a Cleveland sports team wins a championship, I will . . .
"prepare for the apocalypse," — Jeremy Grigsby, Akron

chapter 2: heartbreak

During Brian Sipe's ten years as Browns' quarterback, he set the team's all-time records for pass completions (1,944), yards (23,713), and touchdowns (154). *(Timothy Culek photo)*

Other aspects of the team made that season special. Quarterback Brian Sipe calmly took the Browns down field late in many games and often put the team in position to win. His 1980 season - in which he was voted the AFC MVP - was perhaps the greatest quarterbacking year in team history. He threw for 4,132 yards and 30 touchdowns. Rookie running back and former Heisman Trophy winner Charles White showed glimpses of greatness. The rest of the offense was loaded with talent - Ozzie Newsome at tight end, the Pruitts at running back, Reggie Rucker and Dave Logan at receiver. The defense, led by coordinator Marty Schottenheimer, surprised teams because few believed it would be a positive factor. "Captain Wacko" Lyle Alzado, Clay Matthews, and Thom Darden anchored the defense, which came off an ugly pre-season that had left many people wondering if the Browns could keep opponents under 50 points each game. They surprised the doubters by holding their opponents on average to under 20 points per game.

The 1980 campaign was one in which improbable finishes became the norm,

surviving the drought: cleveland sports fans since 1964

Ozzie Newsome, who in 13 seasons with the Browns, set the team's record for most career receptions and receiving yards, stretches for a touchdown catch against the Bengals. Ozzie was a key part of the excitement which the Kardiac Kids brought. *(Cleveland Stadium Corporation photo, Cleveland Landmarks Press Collection)*

starting with breathtaking defensive stands as time ran out against the Kansas City Chiefs in the third week. The late-game offensive heroics began in week six against Green Bay as Sipe hit Logan with 16 seconds left for a touchdown that clinched a comeback 27-21 victory. Hosting Pittsburgh the following week, the Browns found themselves down 20-7 in the third quarter, only to claw their way back to snag a 27-26 win.

In the second match-up with the arch-rival Steelers in Pittsburgh, the story was almost the same. With 1:44 remaining and the Browns clinging to a 13-9 lead, Terry Bradshaw led the Steelers down the field late in the game and with eleven seconds to play found Lynn Swann in the end zone for a 16-13 win.

The other story that day? Browns' kicker Don Cockroft, who had been battling a bad back, missed three field goals and one extra point. That's right. Ten points. The Browns lost by three in Pittsburgh in a game that could have brought The Jinx to an end. Instead, the Browns trotted off the Three Rivers turf winless for the 11th consecutive year.

Brutal.

Yet other games that year offered a vibrant hope for greater things to come, such as the victory against the Houston Oilers in Texas that put the Browns in control of the division race. The Earl Campbell- and Ken Stabler-led Oilers were stuffed by the Browns, 17-14, in a game that featured Clarence Scott intercepting the ball as the Oilers drove with less than two minutes left in the game. The victory lifted the Browns to 9-4, and with the Browns leading the division so late in the season, fans responded with amazing enthusiasm. The victory over Houston notwithstanding, the Browns

chapter 2: heartbreak

Browns' fans jam the concourse at Cleveland Hopkins International Airport as they await the return of the team after its 1980 victory over the Oilers. The fans were determined that this would be the year.
(Cleveland Press *Collection of the Cleveland State University Libraries)*

had not yet clinched the title, and they still had three games to play. No matter.

The Browns' flight home that Sunday after Thanksgiving was to arrive at Cleveland Hopkins International Airport just after 11:00 p.m., but fans started to arrive at the airport terminal by 9:00 p.m. Within an hour, the concourse was jammed, as thousands of fans awaited the arrival of the Kardiac Kids. These weren't just some fans waiting to cheer; these were fanatics needing to bask in the glory of victory, however transient it might prove. In the concourse, as the temperature leaped, some fainted, but most simply screamed. Outside, traffic was backed up for miles.

When the Browns finally arrived and began to depart the plane, chaos ensued. Fans rushed down the ramp into the plane. They cheered. They screamed. They sang songs. They took pictures of the players and with them.

Darden, who had played in the Rose Bowl with Michigan, had never seen anything like it. "To see the enthusiasm and the way people responded was indescribable," he said.

Hopkins' officials calculated the crowd that greeted the Browns as the airport's second largest gathering - the only one larger being in 1966 when the Beatles came to Cleveland. Remember, the team had not yet won its division title.

The Browns and their fans had to wait three more weeks to celebrate a division championship and a trip to the playoffs. The Browns geared up to face Cincinnati in the Queen City and needed a win to make it to the postseason. The most important part of the game, as usual, was the final two minutes, as the Browns drove downfield with the score tied at 24. With 1:25 remaining, Cockroft kicked the go-ahead field goal.

The fans of the Kardiac Kids seemed to be everywhere in 1980, and the squad became the toast of the town. The sign captures the sentiment that still exists for fans today.
(Cleveland Press Collection of the Cleveland State University Libraries)

But then the Bengals took over. With eight seconds left, quarterback Ken Anderson hit Cincinnati receiver Steve Kreider at the 13-yard line. Six seconds remained. Browns' safety Ron Bolton tackled Kreider, and there were four seconds left. As the Bengals rushed downfield to try to stop the clock, those final four seconds ticked off, and the Browns, in characteristic heart-stopping fashion, emerged as Central Division champions.

The evening of the Browns' victory over the Bengals, an estimated 15,000-18,000 fans gathered at the IX Center to welcome the team home. Fans, who braved traffic snarls and an 11-degree chill, started arriving at 5:30 p.m. in anticipation of their 7:50 p.m. arrival.

The excitement the Kardiac Kids brought to each game helped capture the enthusiasm of a struggling city. Going into the team's first playoff game in eight years, Clevelanders went crazy with Browns' mania.

Thom Darden, who grew up in nearby Sandusky, Ohio, reflected on the effect the 1980 team had on Clevelanders:

> It's not like we're finding a cure for cancer or anything to better society. But then you realize there are people who significantly feel what you're doing. People who get through you a sense of belonging. Then you understand why that entertainment is so important, because a lot of these people did not have positive things in their lives that they could attach themselves to. (*Kardiac Kids*, 219)

For 13 days Clevelanders were transfixed by the Browns. The city seemed to be reborn. Bolstered by the famous "The Twelve Days of a Cleveland Browns

chapter 2: heartbreak

With Brian Sipe at the helm, the Kardiac Kids brought excitement to Browns' fans who had spent the last decade dealing with mediocre play and who had not enjoyed a playoff appearance since 1972.
(Cleveland Stadium Corporation photo, Cleveland Landmarks Press collection)

Christmas" song that seemed to play on radio stations every ten minutes, fans throughout the area hung signs, decorated statues, bought Browns' merchandise, and called sports talk shows to weigh in on the excitement. In some instances, when members of the team were dining out, they were told to leave through the kitchen because swarms of fans wanted to meet them.

By the time of the playoff game with the Oakland Raiders on Jan. 4, 1981, the city had reached a near-fever pitch, despite the fact that the temperature that day dropped to -35 degrees with the wind chill. In a game that featured players wearing "broom ball shoes" with little suction cups on the bottoms, it was no wonder that the first half of the game featured little movement in any direction.

By the end of the third quarter, the Browns held on to a slim 12-7 lead. But then the Raiders offense found a groove for the first time that afternoon. They drove down the field and punched the ball in on a Mark Van Eeghan run which put the Raiders up 14-12.

When the Browns got the ball at their own 28, 4:39 showed on the clock, and it seemed like the same script. Except this time, Sipe fumbled, and the crowd fell silent. Instead of the offense pulling last-minute heroics, it was the defense who stepped in. After three straight Van Eaghan runs which gained nine yards, the Raiders decided to go for it on fourth and one. Van Eaghan was hammered at the line. The Browns held. First down at their own 16 with 2:22 on the clock.

Sipe directed the brown and orange toward the end zone in the open end of Municipal Stadium, and with 49 seconds left, the Browns called time out as the ball rested on the 14-yard line.

surviving the drought: cleveland sports fans since 1964

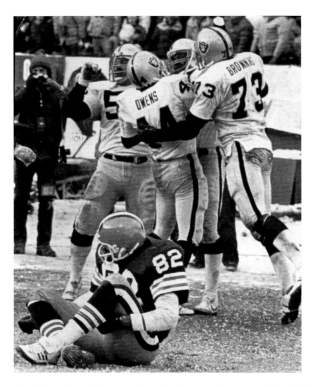

Moments after the most exciting Browns' season in a decade came to an end, Ozzie Newsome, the Browns' Hall of Fame tight end, sits dejected while Oakland players celebrate their playoff victory.
*(Cleveland **Press** Collection of the Cleveland State University Libraries)*

In the huddle on the sidelines, Sipe urged a field goal attempt. Cockroft, though, had already missed two field goals and an extra point, and his season statistics were not much better. Head coach Sam Rutigliano made the call, "Red slot right, halfback stay, 88," and told Sipe that if the primary receiver, Newsome, was covered, to throw it into Lake Erie. When the Browns huddled, Sipe changed the call slightly to "Red right 88, halfback stay" and he envisioned Dave Logan as the primary receiver in the right side of the end zone.

When the ball was snapped, Sipe faded back and unloaded a pass to Newsome, who seemed to have broken away from his defender. Sipe didn't see a wide-open Logan in the end zone, as the play was supposed to develop. As the wobbly ball made it to the end zone, Sipe was swallowed by the Oakland linebackers and could only listen for the result. What he heard was silence.

In the end zone, defender Mike Davis had closed on the receiver, stepped in front of a slipping Newsome, and the ball fell into his arms. The crowd went silent. Newsome lay on the ground, Logan dropped to his knees in the end zone, and Brian Sipe, the loneliest man in Cleveland, picked himself up from the frozen tundra and trotted off the field. When he got to the sideline, Sipe was stunned to hear from Rutigliano, "I love you, Brian."

The miracle finishes were over. The

The next time a Cleveland sports team wins a championship, I will . . .
"be in shock," — Sharon Wieclaw, Akron

chapter 2: heartbreak

Bernie Kosar was a Cleveland favorite during his nine years with the Browns. His having made it known that he wanted to be a Brown brought him instant acceptance, and his leadership and gritty play only added to his popularity. His controversial demotion in 1993 was a blow to his many fans.
(Cleveland Stadium Corporation photo, Cleveland Landmarks Press collection)

first promising, exciting Cleveland sports season in years ended in shock. There was no comeback.

Unfortunately, that wind-swept, snow-choked day would not be matched in anticipation for some years, and in the interim many things changed. Sipe departed for the USFL's New Jersey General in 1983. Gone were running backs Greg Pruitt (ironically, to the Raiders for a short stint) and Mike Pruitt, the receiver corps, the defense, and head coach Sam Rutigliano, who left midway during the 1984 season.

In their place came new players and coaches. By 1985, Marty Schottenheimer was the head coach. Kevin Mack and Earnest Byner anchored the backfield, and both powered their way to 1,000-yard seasons. Bernie Kosar, picked up through a special supplemental draft (which existed for two years to lure players away from the rival USFL), was at quarterback. The Boardman native and University of Miami star had declared openly that he wanted to be a Cleveland Brown. A new, young, aggressive defense took shape, led by safety Don Rogers, cornerbacks Frank Minnefield and Hanford Dixon, and anchored on the line by St. Joseph High School graduate Bob Golic.

The new squad put together an 8-8 record in 1985, allowing them to squeak into the playoffs. That game would sadly, again, end in a sort of heartbreak - not the last-minute variety - but the supremely frustrating, fall-apart performance. On January 4, 1986, the team headed to sunny Miami to face Dan Marino and Don Schula's Dolphins. After the Browns had built up a 21-3 lead, Marino humbled them and directed the Dolphins to a 24-21 win.

Granted, few had predicted postseason success for the .500 Browns, but the

Defensive tackle Jerry Sherk was a stalwart performer for the Browns for 12 seasons. His play, particularly his sack ability, earned him many fans. Sherk's Jerks were always ready to cheer him on, even during the grim 1970s, before the Browns would become serious contenders again in the 1980s. *(Cleveland* Press *Collection of the Cleveland State University Libraries)*

loss was still difficult to bear. One fan, Dex Stuggs of LaGrange remembers taping the game because he wanted to have it in his archives for future viewing.

"After they lost, I would watch the game until Byner scored his touchdown, then turn it off." Did he ever watch the entire game? "No. I preferred to freeze my image of them leading 21-3. Why watch it all? So I can pull out my hair?"

The next Browns' season was generally good for hair growth. However, it was not all good, as the team had suffered a devastating setback when just before training camp was to open, Don Rogers died from a cocaine overdose at his bachelor party. Many players that season wore Rogers' number 20 on their wristbands or the backs of their helmets.

Bolstered by a maturing squad of players, the Browns posted a 12-4 mark, their best winning percentage in 20 years, entitling them to a place in the playoffs where they managed a first-game 23-20 double-overtime victory over the Jets - one of the greatest comeback performances by any team in NFL history. That put them into the Conference final game against the Denver Broncos. Excitement and hope had returned to Cleveland.

Jim Donovan, WKYC's sports director and longtime voice of the Cleveland Browns, had just come to Cleveland as a young sportscaster, and he remembered fondly the build-up to the AFC Championship in January 1987.

"In the week leading up to the game, the entire city was painted orange and brown. Helmets were on statues all over the city. I would drive up and down neighborhood streets, and every house seemed to be decorated," he said. "I grew up in Boston, and they had nothing like this - it was like the city put on a week-

chapter 2: heartbreak

Quarterback Bernie Kosar led the Browns during many of their most exciting playoff seasons. He holds the Browns' records for most all-time playoff passes (260), yards (1,860), and touchdowns (15). *(Cleveland Stadium Corporation photo, Cleveland Landmarks Press Collection)*

long pep rally. It was unbelievable."

Unfortunately, the Browns' faithful couldn't stop time 54:17 into the 1986 AFC Championship game. It was at that precise moment that the diminutive Brian Brennan hauled in a Kosar pass, danced around Denver defensive back Dennis Smith, and trotted in for a 48-yard touchdown catch. Perhaps if the outcome would have been different, the play might have been known as "The Catch," but instead it only meant the Browns were up, 20-13. For a game that had largely been a defensive struggle, many people probably assumed the Brennan score would be the determining factor in the game. Instead, John Elway became the determining factor.

Browns' fans can ask a ton of questions of what became known as "The Drive." What if, on third and two on the Denver 10-yard line, Sammy Winder doesn't get exactly two yards? What if, on third and 18, Mark Jackson doesn't haul in a 20-yard pass? It hurts too much to review, but those things did happen, and Elway led the Broncos downfield against the Browns defense. With 37 seconds remaining, Jackson grabbed a pass in the Dawg Pound endzone to tie the game and to silence the Municipal Stadium throng. Many forget

surviving the drought: cleveland sports fans since 1964

Brian Brennan catches a Bernie Kosar pass for a fourth-quarter touchdown in the 1987 AFC championship game at Cleveland Stadium. This is the closest the Browns ever came to reaching the Super Bowl, just before John Elway started "The Drive." *(Cleveland Browns photo, Cleveland Landmarks Press collection)*

that the Browns won the coin toss in overtime, and many forget that on the third play of that opening overtime drive, the Browns couldn't convert on third and two. In some ways, the deflation of the Denver touchdown, of Elway's heroic efforts, was almost too much to overcome. It was as if overtime was simply a formality. And in fact, it became that.

The faithful fans, basking in the intense excitement of the Brennan touchdown, knew they had witnessed the nearest the Browns had come to a Super Bowl trip since the big game had started. After the referees signaled Rich Karlis' field goal kick "good," the crowd simply couldn't leave. They immediately sent the team a tremendous cheer for the thrills they had been treated to, and many stayed in the bleachers and the rest of the Stadium long after the 23-20 loss. Some who were there, like Dave Sartorius of Norwalk, took the difficult blow in stride. He told The *Plain Dealer*, "It's the ups and downs of sports . . . life goes on tomorrow." Some had a harder time of it. John Zorich of Strongsville said, "I'm damned tired of saying 'next year.' I wanted it now."

Bud Dreier couldn't tear himself away from the depressing scene. "We stayed in the Stadium until it was almost empty and took a picture of the scoreboard. How sad."

The next time a Cleveland sports team wins a championship, I will . . .
"get a tattoo of the team's logo like I did when the Indians went to the World Series in '95," — Bud Dreier, Akron

chapter 2: heartbreak

After the Denver Broncos defeated the Browns 23-20 in overtime in the 1987 AFC title game, all that remained was trash — and more heartbreak for Cleveland fans.
(Diana McNees photo, Cleveland Public Library collection)

It should come as no surprise that most fans interviewed referred to "The Drive" as the most disappointing moment in Cleveland sports.

Donovan remembers the drastic change from the excited anticipation before the game to the moments after the game.

"It was unbelievably quiet, despondent, silent," he said. "You couldn't hear yourself in the city for one week, but at 4:30 p.m. on that Sunday, you could hear a pin drop."

At the time of the Browns' implosion, could Cleveland devotees have known what was in store for them over the next few years? One year after Elway damaged Cleveland fans' psyches, the veteran Browns walked into Denver for an AFC Championship game rematch. What happened? Well, to put it into current context, Peyton Manning orchestrated the best comeback in AFC Championship game history when in 2007 he led the Colts from a 21-3 halftime deficit against the New England Patriots to propel Indianapolis into the big show, 38-34. Had the January 1988 AFC Championship game gone differently, Manning might have tied another quarterback for the greatest comeback of all time. Tied Bernie Kosar, that is.

surviving the drought: cleveland sports fans since 1964

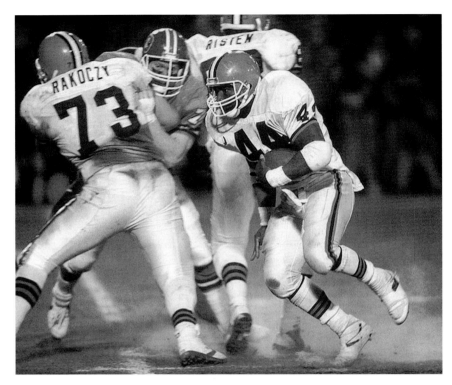

It would be nice to stop time right about now. Byner looked for the goal line just before Jeremiah Castille caused "The Fumble." *(Richard Mackson photo*, Sports Illustrated*)*

Ifs, buts, candies, nuts.

In the AFC Championship rematch in Denver, a sloppy first-half performance left the Browns down 21-3, and the ghosts of Cleveland sports moments past seemed to loom large until Earnest Byner and Kosar ignited the offense in the second half. Putting together drives that almost buried all the past frustrations, the second-half Browns seemed unstoppable. The pace of scoring was furious - Kosar passed for four touchdowns in the second half alone. Elway and the Broncos kept pace until the score read 38-31 with five minutes left in the game. And with 1:12 left on the clock and the Browns standing at the eight-yard line, it seemed the demons might be put to rest. Instead, as fans know, Byner went left off tackle, saw daylight, and neared the goal line. He made it into the endzone, but the ball did not, and "The Fumble," incredibly, became yet another defining and depressing moment in Cleveland sports memories.

Most fans don't count the play as the most gut-wrenching in Cleveland sports history because Byner was trying to tie the game, the Browns had seemed out of it for such a big part of the game, and the Broncos' offense in the second half seemed as unstoppable as the Browns'. No matter. The desperation sounded more loudly that year.

"Two bleeping years in a row," said Bob Schultz of Toledo to The *Plain Dealer*. "We lost, we lost, we lost . . ."

Joe Wolfe of North Olmsted took it a little further. While acknowledging his pain for Byner, he simply said, " . . . I feel like I want to kill."

Some simply admitted to throwing in the proverbial towel during the game because it was so intense. One woman who was at a party in Cleveland Heights

chapter 2: heartbreak

Starting in 1973, John Adams began going to Tribe games. Since then, he continues to bang his drum, having lived through the "Pass," "The Drive," "The Fumble," "The Shot," Game 7, and all the other Cleveland sports miseries. In 2006 the Indians rewarded him by dedicating a fan "giveaway" (bobble arms) to him – the only time the team has ever honored a specific fan. *(Cleveland* Press *photo, Cleveland Landmarks Press collection)*

said, "a couple of us switched to hard liquor after the first quarter." And it wasn't as if Cleveland devotees could escape the hangover the next day, as the pain continued - for years.

At least for Clevelanders that fall and winter, the 1988-89 Cavaliers seemed to offer hope. The end of that tale, sadly, was yet another storied shocker that sent waves of pain through the Cleveland faithful. That event became known simply as "The Shot," courtesy of the Chicago Bulls' Michael Jordan, and well, it seemed more like a shotgun blast.

What made Jordan's heroics even more difficult to bear was the fact that the Bulls had ended the Cavs' season the year before in a best-of-five playoff series. But the 1988-89 Cavs had matured under the leadership of head coach Lenny Wilkens to the tune of 15 more wins than the 1987-88 squad. They finished the campaign with an impressive 57-25 record, a franchise best. Their core players that year had gelled impressively - Brad Daugherty, Ron Harper, Mark Price, Larry Nance, and John "Hot Rod" Williams - and Cleveland fans gladly went along for the ride.

In the fifth, deciding game of the opening playoff series in Cleveland on May 7, the game came down to the one player everyone expected it would. The Cavs led the entire game. With a few seconds left, however, the Bulls grabbed a 99-98 lead. After a timeout, Craig Ehlo - who had sat for two games in the series with an ankle injury, ending his ironman-like streak of starts that had endured for six years - seemed to emerge the hero. After inbounding the ball and then getting it back, he sliced through the Chicago D to net a lay-up on a perfectly executed give-and-go that put the Cavs up 100-99 with three seconds left.

surviving the drought: cleveland sports fans since 1964

Though Cleveland fans have come to expect heartbreaks rather than euphoria when they attend a game, occasionally, though not quite frequently enough, they get to see a gem, like Lenny Barker's May 15, 1981, perfect game. Here Cleveland police escort him from the field after the game.
(Western Reserve Historical Society collection)

In the huddle, Chicago head coach Doug Collins told the team to get Jordan the ball and then get the "%#*@ out of the way." His star got the ball, drew up for a jumper at the free throw line, seemed to escape for a split second the pull of gravity that keeps most people tethered close to the ground, and released a shot over the outstretched arms of Ehlo, one of the Cavs' best defenders that year. You know the story: the return of Jordan to the hardwood floor, the deafening silence in the Coliseum, the arm-pump of the player who would become known as the greatest to ever have his sneakers squeak on an NBA court.

The Pass. The Drive. The Fumble. The Shot. What would be next?

The Move.

Ask Cleveland sports fans about some of the lowest moments in the history of their devotion, and surely the year 1995 rears its ugly head. Not because the Indians, for the first time since 1954, made it to the World Series, only to lose in six games to the Atlanta Braves. No - because many fans were still excited that the team had actually won the American League pennant and made it to the World Series. And, frankly, most experts and observers predicted that the pitching-loaded Braves would win the title. But, nine days after the Indians went home as the second-best team in baseball, nine days after the Indians came the closest any Cleveland

The next time a Cleveland sports team wins a championship, I will . . .
"be six feet under," — Chris Stupica, Hudson

chapter 2: heartbreak

Although Browns' fans had to do without their beloved team for three NFL seasons, they fought to secure a team that took the field again in 1999. Since then, they have been able to resume their love affair.
(Ron Kuntz photo)

team had come to winning a championship since 1964, Browns' owner Art Modell announced that he was moving the Browns to Baltimore.

Talk about cruel.

On Nov. 6, 1995, Modell sat on a stage in Baltimore to announce his move of a team that had established itself in a city that had come to adore it. In the meantime, he had sent a moving company to pack up the organization's materials, an act reminiscent of Robert Irsay, the Baltimore Colts' owner who stole the team out from under the Baltimore fans one night in 1984 and showed up in Indianapolis. The debate about who was to blame for the shocking news ensued. Most fans blamed Modell for taking the financially strapped team out from under the city's nose, but some also saw the fault belonging to the City for not treating the Browns as they had done the Indians and Cavs in the years leading up to 1995. Those teams had received state-of-the-art new venues in which to play. The Browns were still in old Municipal Stadium, and the city had turned a cold shoulder to Modell's proposals to update the facility.

Whatever the case, a sports tradition was ripped from Cleveland, despite numerous lawsuits by fans against Modell. Fans took the announcement so seriously that they even traveled to Washington, D.C., and implored NFL Commissioner Paul Tagliabue to keep the team where the tradition had begun. Cleveland Mayor Mike White, who adopted the slogan, "no team, no peace," helped lead an effort that eventually forced the NFL to leave behind the Browns' colors (which Modell hated anyway) and traditions (mainly records). Most importantly, the mayor helped secure an NFL commitment to an

There was something amazing about a full Municipal Stadium – especially when more than 70,000 fans took in a baseball game. The roar of the crowd was distinctive in the cavernous "Lady by the Lake."
(Cleveland Stadium Corporation photo, Cleveland Landmarks Press)

expansion franchise that would return to a Cleveland field in 1999. But the damage had been done.

In Cleveland, the shock reverberated like no other event in the area's sports history. In some corners, anger flowed like hot lava. Dante Lavelli gave a profanity-laced interview in *Sports Illustrated*, but the magazine didn't print the obscenities. When he had finally calmed down, he tried to capture what the move meant to the Rust Belt City that had been belted by the news.

"This isn't just football that's being taken away. It's a part of people's lives," Lavelli said.

Tears gushed from the eyes of the thousands who had gone hoarse in the Dawg Pound, shared moments with fathers in their living rooms, hollered at the players, leapt with excitement, and went to bed dreaming of a hoped-for championship. It was almost unbearable, because for so many, there was no zone of psychological comfort. There wasn't even that empty feeling so many had experienced at the very end of each Browns' season, expressed in so many ways, since 1964, but always amounting to: "at least there's next year." An identity had been ripped apart, and a city's flocking faithful had been brought to their knees.

chapter 2: heartbreak

When Kenny Lofton began his nine-year career with the Indians, they were still playing at Municipal Stadium, and the fans were hoping for some excitement. Lofton provided that with his hitting, his fielding, and his base stealing. He is the Indians' all-time base stealer. *(Skip Trombetti photo)*

As Lou "The Toe" Groza said in *Sports Illustrated*, "It's like a fire has just burned out, and all you're left with is ashes."

And smoldering resentment. Cleveland Browns' fans could rightly point to their unconditional love. For instance, from 1990-1994, when the team's combined record was 34-46, the fans averaged sixth in the league in attendance. From 1975 until the announcement, the team had put together seven playoff runs and three appearances in the AFC championship game - not exactly stellar success over 20 years - and in those 20 years, the Browns ranked second or third in league attendance 11 times.

From those bleak December days of 1995, and into those eerily quiet autumn Sundays in 1996, Cleveland sports fans struggled. For a short time, there would be one less professional team that could break fans' hearts. And yet, that's just what happened during the Browns' hiatus, although it's hard to classify as a heartbreaker the 1997 Indians' playoff run.

Sure, they lost the World Series. Sure, the world championship slipped from their grasp in the ninth inning of the seventh game of the World Series. Sure, the Florida Marlins became champions, despite the fact that they were a five-year-old team loaded with high-priced free agent talent which basically disbanded within a few months of their World Series victory.

It was only a heartbreaker because the Indians pulled off the most impressive postseason run in Cleveland sports history and made it to a big show they were never really invited to. Prognosticators had not picked the 1997 squad to do especially well in the postseason, despite the fact that everyone predicted them to walk away with the AL Central Division title - then regarded by most as the weakest

surviving the drought: cleveland sports fans since 1964

A huge crowd in Public Square cheer the 1995 American League champion Indians, the city's first pennant winner since 1954, and wish them luck in the World Series. The rally proved insufficient, however, as the Braves defeated the Tribe 4-2. *(Ron Kuntz photo)*

division in baseball. Nor did the 1997 Tribe dispel such concerns, as at times their play seemed lackluster.

They were a team of aging veterans - some who showed up for only a short time (like Julio Franco) and some who joined the team in the latter part of the season (Kevin Seitzer). They were a team of pitchers struggling to keep their combined ERA under 4.50. They were a team that tallied a ho-hum 86 victories. And, in the postseason, of the eight teams that qualified for the playoffs, the Tribe had the second-worst regular season record and the worst record among the four American League postseason squads.

Then, consider the fact that in the short division series against the New York Yankees, the Tribe traveled to the Bronx, promptly put up five runs in the top of the first inning of the first game, and then let the game slip away, 8-6.

But from the second game of the division series onward, the 1997 Tribe played as if guided by some magical source. The team could have quietly gone away in the eight-team race for the World Series championship, but instead Cleveland fans were treated to a string of incredible games that rank as some of the finest experiences in Cleveland sports history.

Ultimately, like all of Cleveland sports experiences of the last 43 years, the Tribe did not capture the 1997 World Series. It didn't help Cleveland fans' fragile and aching sports' psyches that the Tribe lost it

The next time a Cleveland sports team wins a championship, I will . . .
"have a heart attack," — John Whitely, Avon

chapter 2: heartbreak

Jim Thome was a key player in the Indians' exciting seasons during the 1990s, and he made it known that he liked Cleveland. He holds the team's all-time career home run record. Fans felt betrayed when he turned down a multi-million dollar offer from the Indians to move to the Phillies in 2003. *(Ron Kuntz photo)*

in extra innings in the seventh game after having led the contest.

But what a ride it was.

In the second game of the division series, the Indians penciled in 21-year-old rookie Jaret Wright to battle 18-game winner Andy Pettite. In a game the Tribe desperately needed, Wright found himself down 3-0 after the first inning. It seemed to many that the 1997 Tribe was going to go the way of those who will inherit the earth: meekly. Then, the tide actually turned in the Indians' favor. Each time Wright exited the dugout for his next trip to the mound, he pitched brilliantly. As if by some sort of miracle, the Indians strung together hits and home runs against Pettite, and the Indians pulled off a split in New York with a 7-5 win.

In the next game at the Jake, David Wells (five-hit complete game) and Paul O'Neill (grand slam) combined to take the Indians within nine innings of elimination with a 6-1 thumping. The Indians in the next game found themselves four outs from cleaning out their lockers for the season. They were down, 2-1, and Mariano Rivera came in to finish them off. Indians' catcher Sandy Alomar, who was having the best season of his life - with

Omar Vizquel was arguably the city's favorite Indian during the great Tribe seasons in the 1990s, and he made it known that he wanted to stay with the team. But management decided otherwise, and he was sent to the Mariners. Cleveland fans have been wounded in many different ways. *(Ron Kuntz photo)*

a regular season average and career-best .320 average, 21 home runs, 83 RBIs, and a game-winning home run at the All-Star game in Jacobs' Field - faced the New York fireballer in the eighth inning.

Amazingly, Alomar's storybook season continued when he popped a 2-0 pitch over the right field wall to tie the score. With momentum on their side, the Indians stepped up to the plate in the ninth inning to scrape one run on a deflected Omar Vizquel hit up the middle that scored Marquis Grissom. In the fifth and deciding game, the Indians again sent Wright out in a high-pressure situation - against Pettite again - and the rookie responded.

The Tribe held on to win, 4-3. It should be noted that in typical nail-biting fashion, the Yanks had the tying run on second in the ninth inning when Jose Mesa was able to get Bernie Williams to fly out to end the game and the series.

In the ALCS, the Tribe dropped the first contest, 3-0. But the Indians didn't surrender, even when in the second game they found themselves down, 4-2. Marquis Grissom hit a three-run home run against Armando Benitez to cap a comeback win and secure a split in Baltimore. Two days later in Jacobs Field, Grissom was at the center of two game-breaking plays in game 3, which featured dominant

chapter 2: heartbreak

Sandy Alomar was a key to the 1997 World Series-bound squad. He had a career year. *(Ron Kuntz photo)*

pitching performances from Orioles' ace Mike Mussina and the Indians' Orel Hershiser. During the pitching duel which ultimately featured 33 combined strikeouts, the Indians clung to a 1-0 lead when with two outs in the ninth inning and a runner on second, a seemingly routine fly ball was sent to Grissom in center. He lost it in the lights and had no idea where it was until alerted by the thud 30 feet behind him. The game was tied.

In the 12th inning of the nail-biter, Grissom stood at third base with one out and Omar Vizquel at the plate. Vizquel attempted to squeeze the runner home, but missed the ball, and Orioles catcher Lenny Webster (who later insisted Vizquel had tipped it) let the ball get away, allowing Grissom to score the winning run.

Fans at Jacobs Field the next evening watched the Tribe claw its way back from a 5-2 deficit and take a 7-5 lead. The Tribe couldn't hold the lead, and in the top of the ninth the Orioles tied it. Then, with two outs in the bottom of the ninth inning, Sandy Alomar, Jr., stepped to the plate and singled home Manny Ramirez from second base. Alomar helped produce another amazing one-run victory that put the Tribe one game from the World Series.

Seemingly everything was going the Tribe's way - even with an Orioles' 4-0

surviving the drought: cleveland sports fans since 1964

Following the ALCS upset of the Orioles, the Indians headed into a World Series that few people predicted would feature the Indians. *(Heinz Kluetmeier*, Sports Illustrated*)*

lead heading into the ninth inning of the fifth game. The way things had gone, it seemed yet another perfect stage for some Indian player to shine. But, it wasn't to be, as the Tribe lost, 4-2. The series stood at 3-2 in favor of the Tribe.

When the series shifted back to Camden Yards for the sixth game, fans were treated to a pitchers' duel. Going into extra innings, no runs had been produced by either team. But then, Tony Fernandez stepped up against Benitez in the top of the 11th inning. With two outs he created yet more magic for the seemingly Hollywood-scripted baseball squad from Cleveland: he sent a 2-0 pitch over the right field wall to break the scoreless tie.

In the bottom of the 11th, with two outs and a runner on, Mesa faced Roberto Alomar, who had ended the Tribe's season the year before on a home run in the Division Series. This time, however, Mesa blazed a third strike past a frozen Alomar, preserving the Indians' second American League Championship in three years.

For many fans, it seemed as if the Cleveland jinx had been suspended, at least thus far. Could it be broken? It seemed entirely possible. In unbelievable fashion the Tribe had defeated two teams they were not supposed to beat, and they did it with heroics not seen from Cleveland teams in decades. In the ALCS, all four Tribe victories were by one run,

The next time a Cleveland sports team wins a championship, I will . . .
"run naked down East Ninth Street," — Rob Shoens, Brunswick

chapter 2: heartbreak

The 1997 Tribe came even closer than the 1995 Indians to honoring the last Cleveland Indians World Series title. (Cleveland Landmarks Press collection)

a new MLB record. Perhaps this was the year, Cleveland fans desperately thought.

Facing the Indians in the 1997 edition of the Fall Classic were the Florida Marlins. In the first game in Florida, the Marlins won 7-4. Then the Indians, behind the solid pitching of Chad Ogea, bounced back to tie the series with a 6-1 victory. When the series moved back to Cleveland, the teams treated the fans to a display which Manager Mike Hargrove called the "ugliest game you'll ever see." Heading into the 9th inning with a 7-7 tie, the Marlins put up 7 runs en route to a 14-11 win.

The Indians tallied ten runs the next night in a frigid Jacobs Field, and Jaret Wright kept the Marlins in check with yet another big win.

In the fifth game, the Tribe took a 4-2 lead heading into the sixth inning, but Moises Alou hit a three-run shot as the Marlins swam past the Indians, 8-4. The Tribe was heading to Florida down three games to two. The next game was a must-win.

The sixth game featured Chad Ogea driving in as many runs as he would need to win the game (two) even though, as he said, he hadn't swung a bat since high school. Helped by amazing defense plays by Omar Vizquel (a two-run-saving out deep in the hole), David Justice (sliding catch), and Marquis Grissom (an over-the-shoulder Willie Mays-like catch of a shot to deep center field), Ogea pitched unflappably. With the Indians on the brink of losing the series, he provided the grist behind the Tribe's 4-1 win.

The seventh and deciding game was played on October 26, 1997. For that one day, Cleveland fans could dream about a World Series championship. For that one day, Cleveland fans asked

surviving the drought: cleveland sports fans since 1964

Another minor heartbreak happened at the end of the 2005 season, when the Indians faced the Chicago White Sox in a bid to make the playoffs. The Tribe was swept from playoff contention, and Sox manager Ozzie Guillen added insult to injury. *(David Richard photo)*

the question: "What will it feel like if the Tribe wins tonight?" For that one day, Cleveland fans played with the idea of putting all their demons to rest - Red Right 88, The Drive, The Fumble, The Shot, The Move - and finding some legitimacy in national sports. For that one day, Cleveland fans could think about how to honor the memory of the thousands of Cleveland sports fans who had died - unfulfilled, no doubt - sometime in the previous 33 years without seeing a championship.

And in truth, what baseball-loving fans in America weren't rooting for the Tribe and its long-suffering fans? True, the 1997 series turned out to be one of the least watched series in baseball history. The early games of the World Series posted viewer ratings 18% below the worst ratings in history, and even Commissioner Bud Selig said "Yes, the ratings would have been higher if Baltimore or even New York would have played Atlanta." Such comments made Marlins' manager Jim Leyland want "to puke," but nevertheless, Cleveland sports fans told themselves that the baseball gods and baseball fans around the country surely had to be pulling for the Indians, as the possibility of ending their long-standing tradition of suffering would be far more heartening than a World Series victory by a five-year-old team loaded with journeymen free agents.

Wright continued his brilliance in the postseason during the seventh game of the series, pitching like a veteran into the seventh inning and leaving the Indians with a 2-1 lead.

Then the ninth inning happened.

As Cleveland fans could taste vindication just two outs away, it happened. It fell apart. The fact that the Indians lost in

chapter 2: heartbreak

And then there was one. Following the last game of the last series during the 2005 Indians' season, a lonely soul considers yet one more lost chance for championship glory. *(David Richard photo)*

the 11th inning was in many ways a formality, as the devastation occurred in the 9th inning when two singles and a sacrifice fly by Craig Counsell scored the tying run. Just like that, the momentum that Wright had provided, the Indians' hopes of slipping out of Miami as World Series champions, went up in a cloud of dust. To make things more gruesomely painful, the baseball gods took a swipe at Tony Fernandez, whose heroics had helped the Tribe get to the championship series. He committed an error on a slow-rolling grounder in the 11th inning that helped to load the bases and allow Edgar Renteria to single home the winning run. The Marlins captured a World Series championship for the first time in their short-storied history.

Clevelanders and the city's sports fans struggled mightily to deal with the wreckage of another near-miss heartbreaker. Stories and columns in The *Plain Dealer* in the following week expressed disappointment in the end result, but typical pride in the team for making it as far as they had. A few days after the game-seven loss, about 50,000 Cleveland fans welcomed the 1997 American League champs with a Public Square rally and reminded the team (and themselves) that all was not lost in the failed bid for the World Series. They applauded the players for their effort and thanked them for the incredible ride. Cleveland fans had become experts at such face-saving and psyche-salving comments after such letdowns.

surviving the drought: cleveland sports fans since 1964

"Bingo" Smith and Bill Fitch take in the last moments of the most historic run the Cavs had experienced in their short history. Their 1976 trip to the Eastern Conference finals was the first for the franchise, and would not be repeated until 1992. *(Cleveland* Press *Collection of the Cleveland State University Libraries)*

But scan the columns and headlines in the wake of the loss, and one would find the depths to which many Clevelanders had plummeted, captured well in many *Plain Dealer* columns with titles such as "Players go through 'nightmare,'" "Welcome to Cleveland, city of unavoidable pain," and "A closed circle of grief." For those who lived and died with Cleveland sports, it was almost too much to bear. Fans and observers sought answers that were not there. They waxed philosophically about how the pain Cleveland fans have endured have made them unique, about how no other fans in the country could understand our anguish. None of it seemed fair in the grand scheme of life. Sadly, in the aftermath, all fans could hope for was time, so that they could remember it as history - not the present. The present, as had so often been the case, was too painful.

It was difficult to find any psychological refuge to ease the pain. How could Cleveland fans dampen the disappointment? They were clueless. They felt like Ray Kinsella in *Field of Dreams*. Hell, if building a baseball field would have been the solution, Cleveland fans would have readily plowed under a field of corn - maybe thousands of fields of corn - in a heartbeat.

But of course it wasn't to be, as none of those other close calls with championship destiny had been. Perhaps, fans were left to wonder, it could only come true in some dreamlike haze illuminated by ghostlike lights somewhere in the middle of nowhere, Iowa.

Who knows?

Because it sure as hell wasn't happening in Cleveland, Ohio.

3 poor judgment
surviving the drought

A word to the wise ain't necessary - it's the stupid ones that need the advice. — Bill Cosby

Let's come clean. While Cleveland sports fans can and should be proud of their intense devotion to their teams, there have been times when that passion has spilled over to produce some utter embarrassments.

The two most obvious examples of collective poor judgment, of course, were the June 4, 1974, Beer Night incident that exploded in the late innings of a game between the Tribe and the Texas Rangers and the beer-bottle throwing incident near the end of the Browns' game against the Jacksonville Jaguars on December 16, 2001.

In the Beer Night incident, a bunch of rowdy drunks - encouraged by the cheap beers they had downed all night - stormed the field of Cleveland Municipal Stadium and went after the Texas Rangers. To put the event into perspective, the 25,134 people in attendance downed approximately 65,000 dime-priced beers. Add to the mix the fact that six days earlier the Tribe and Rangers had nearly experienced a bench-clearing brawl in Texas, and the evening seemed to be brewed with bad behavior just waiting to happen.

Yet, the infamous ninth-inning incident that featured players from both the Cleveland Indians and Texas Rangers fighting for their lives against unruly fans was in fact the culmination of a situation that had been descending into chaos the entire evening. Throughout that warm June evening at Cleveland Municipal Stadium, fans repeatedly displayed poor judgment. From a pre-game scuffle between a beer vendor and a fan, to nearly constant interruptions in play because of fans running out onto the field, the game slowly slipped into disaster.

Once, as the Texas Rangers' DH Tom Grieve circled the bases in the fourth

surviving the drought: cleveland sports fans since 1964

Most baseball fans like to try to catch foul balls. The ball was too far behind this fan, but Baltimore's Eddie Murray did get a head. *(Ron Kuntz photo)*

inning after his second home run of the game, a male fan ran and slid into second base while Grieve was still on the base path. Another doozy featured a father and son who sprinted to the outfield and double-mooned the fans. As the heat of the summer day burned off late in the game, some fans decided to turn up the temperature in their own special way. Around the seventh inning, some started hurling firecrackers at the Texas relief pitchers in the visitors' bullpen. Near the end of the game, groups of fans started to run onto the field, perform stupid antics, and then sprint back into the stands.

Finally, in the ninth inning, Texas right fielder Jeff Burroughs was standing in the outfield when a fan jumped the wall, ran up behind him, and stole his cap. Burroughs spun to get his hat back, but slipped. Not knowing from the dugout what had happened to Burroughs - just seeing that he had gone down and a fan had just run up to him - Rangers' Manager Billy Martin came charging out of the dugout wielding a baseball bat with orders for his players to go with him.

Sensing an oncoming riot, Cleveland manager Ken Aspromonte followed Martin's lead, and sent his players - with bats in hand - to help the Texas Rangers defend themselves. Two teams who less than a week before had been on the verge of killing each other joined forces to

The next time a Cleveland sports team wins a championship, I will . . .
"probably watch downtown Cleveland be destroyed. We won't know what to do with ourselves," — Peggy Schauer, North Ridgeville

chapter 3: poor judgment

Beer night ended in an Indians' forfeit. Getting toasted seemed to many fans to be the worth the price of admission when the hopes of the Indians' arising from their prolonged baseball miseries seemed a long shot. *(Ron Kuntz photo)*

defend themselves against a few hundred drunks, some of whom wielded knives, chains, and pieces of stadium seats. For a few minutes, fights raged, and chaos reigned. Players and umpires fought to escape unharmed.

The ninth-inning disturbance lasted only a few minutes. The game was called, and ironically enough and in typical Cleveland fashion - only after the Indians had come back from a 5-1 deficit and tied it in the ninth before the game was interrupted; the Indians officially lost the game as a forfeit.

WJW's Dan Coughlin remembers being at that game as a reporter and watching the spectacle. After the game had been forfeited, he found about 20 high school kids standing on top of the visitors' dugout, seemingly challenging any of the Rangers to come out to fight. Some players were still in the dugout, but others were in the clubhouse.

"So I jump on top of the dugout with my notebook, and I ask, 'What are you trying to accomplish?' They turned to look at me, and one kid out of nowhere just punches me in the jaw."

Almost 20 years later, Coughlin took his own children to an Indians' game, and lo and behold, one of those kids from the top of the dugout during Beer Night noticed Coughlin in the stands.

Coughlin continued, "He comes up to me with a friend and says, 'You remember beer night? This is the guy who punched you.' He was a guy who went to Cathedral Latin, and he was there with his own little son, and I'm thinking 'wouldn't he be proud of you now?'"

In truth, though the Beer Night incident was brief, it had a long-lasting impact on how others viewed Cleveland and its sports fans. As the years went on, observers would often refer to the "passion"

surviving the drought: cleveland sports fans since 1964

Rangers' manager Billy Martin makes it clear to the umpires just what he thinks of the situation in Cleveland Stadium during the Beer Night fiasco.
(Ron Kuntz photo)

of Cleveland sports fans. What they noticed was one small segment of the Cleveland sports nation collectively becoming demented.

Over time, the Cleveland faithful would get some treats that allowed them to show off their intense devotion in more acceptable ways. The 1976 miracle Cavaliers made it to the playoffs. In 1980, the Kardiac Kids gave fans a chance to go berserk. Then an unlikely guest made it to Cleveland in the mid-to-late 1980s: Success. It came especially for the Browns, who made the playoffs in 1985, and then for the rest of the decade became a fixture in the late-season dance. It also came in a minor way for the Indians in 1986, when they had their best won-loss record since 1965 (although still finishing in fifth place) and for the Cavs who made it to the playoffs in the 1987-1988 season and followed up with eight more appearances in the next nine years.

But with success also came some rather raucous behavior, most notably that which was seen in the Dawg Pound, the bleacher area in Municipal Stadium during Browns' games that became known for a regular contingent of drunkards, fighters, ex-cons, and maybe even a few convicts who slipped out of jail just to attend. You can imagine some of what followed, even though the events may not be as ignominious as Beer Night.

One incident occurred during a 1988 game against the Houston Oilers. After a cameraman stationed near the Dawg Pound was knocked unconscious in a collision with some players, fans began to throw snowballs at the man prostrate on the sidelines. Truly an embarrassment for all decent Cleveland sports fans.

chapter 3: poor judgment

The Dawg Pound has been home to the most rabid of Browns' fans. While from time to time there has been some rowdy behavior there, mostly the Pound's clientele devoted themselves to bellowing out their support for the team.
(Cleveland Stadium Corporation photo, Cleveland Landmarks Press Collection)

In the era of the Dawg Pound - between 1985 and 1995 - officials stopped two Browns' games because they were concerned that the dog bones, biscuits, and batteries that were hurled from the stands might injure players. The games (one against Houston, the other Denver) had to be halted to allow the opposing teams to receive a new placement of the ball, allowing them to drive toward the closed end of the field.

As if that weren't bad enough, Cleveland fans' reputation became more permanently etched in popular imagination when in 1989 Sam Wyche, then the head coach of the Cincinnati Bengals, grabbed the public address microphone at Cincinnati's Riverfront Stadium near the end of a Bengals' game against the Seattle Seahawks. Some of the Bengals' faithful had begun firing snowballs at the area around which the Seahawks' placekicker was about to attempt a game-winning field goal. In Wyche's famously shouted words, he reminded them, "You don't live in Cleveland. You live in Cincinnati!"

Although many outsiders and Cleveland sports fans acknowledge that the scene for fans at the new Browns Stadium is not very much like it was on game day in Municipal Stadium, there have been more recent displays of poor judgment, including the other major event in Cleveland sports history that made many Clevelanders, and others around the country, wince. That event was the famous beer-bottle-throwing incident at the end of the Browns-Jacksonville game on December 16, 2001.

The brown and orange, led by Tim Couch, had been driving toward a winning touchdown late in the game when Quincy Morgan caught a pass inside the Jaguars' 10-yard line with less than a

61

"Yo Butch Make Us Proud!" some Cleveland fans declared as they pelted members of the grounds crew and of the Browns and Jaguars with full and empty beer bottles, cameras, binoculars, and anything else they could find. Yes, make us proud. *(David Richard photo)*

minute left. Quickly, Couch spiked the next snap to stop the clock. The referees then decided to review the supposed catch by Morgan - despite NFL rules that state that no play can be reviewed after another play has been run. The refs disallowed the catch, turning the ball and the contest over to Jacksonville. As if Cleveland sports fans hadn't been feeling for decades that the stars had been aligned against them, now they actually suffered a referee crew who broke the league's own rules to punch the Browns in the gut.

Although the officials later claimed they had signaled for a review in time, many fans would hear nothing of it. They hurled virtually anything they could get their hands on toward the officials, who tried to duck for cover. Fans chiefly tossed food and plastic beer bottles - some full and some not - but there were reports of other, more dangerous projectiles, and they didn't come from fans in just the first few rows near the field. Some came from individuals hidden in the upper rows. There were reports that even cameras and binoculars came raining down onto people in the stands and onto the field.

After the game, although Browns' president Carmen Policy seemed to dismiss the behavior (later he would apologize for not condemning the actions more harshly), some thought the passion was fairly impressive.

Tim Couch said in an interview afterward that while he was standing with some Jacksonville players at mid-field during the barrage of bottles, the Jaguar players told Couch, "I wish our fans were as into it as your fans are."

Yes, that's apparently how some people would describe Cleveland fans launching full beer bottles out of rage. "Into it."

At the end of the 2005 season, an-

chapter 3: poor judgment

Near the end of the Steelers' drubbing of the Browns in 2005, Steelers' linebacker James Harrison slammed Browns' fan Nathan Mallett to the turf - an embarrassing exclamation point to a brutal afternoon. *(David Richard photo)*

other showing of questionable judgment jumped onto TV screens and into newspapers around the country. Near the end of a horrific 41-0 Steelers' drubbing of the Browns in Browns Stadium, 24-year old Nathan Mallett - ironic last name - decided to show his displeasure at the spectacle (or maybe just to demonstrate how many beers he had downed) by bolting out onto the turf. Mallett chose to dance around on the field for a short time, where he was pushed by the Browns' Kennard Lang before Steelers' linebacker James Harrison came up from behind, and slammed Mallett onto the turf. After he upended the drunken fan, he knelt over him, and held him down until the police could arrest him.

Three days later, Judge Joan Synenberg, who had to deal with punishing Mallett, decided to hammer her gavel at Mallett. Apparently not convinced by his not guilty plea, and in order to "send a message," she ordered him jailed for the weekend of the 2006 Super Bowl, where he would not have any access to the game. That was just one part of her message. She also slapped him with a $400 fine, 150 hours of community service, and, probably the kicker of all, a ban from Browns' games for five years.

More often than not, it has been Browns' fans, who during the heat of battle, have been the ones to demonstrate some out-of-line behaviors. For Indians' fans, there have been fewer well-publicized incidents outside the Beer Night fiasco, but there have been some.

In 1991, a young Albert Belle made headlines when he gunned a ball into the chest of a heckling fan at Municipal Stadium. Belle had just decided to return to his given name of Albert instead of the name he had been using - Joey - and had

surviving the drought: cleveland sports fans since 1964

It is not only fans who can show occasional poor judgment. Albert Belle, who spent eight years with the Indians, garnered headlines for his bat as well as for his temper.
(Skip Trombetti photo)

just spent a part of the previous season in alcohol rehabilitation. He was trotting off the field when a particularly gutsy fan named Jeff Pillar yelled to him, "Hey Joey, keg party at my place after the game."

Belle picked up a ball, and from 15 feet away, amazingly, struck Pillar squarely in the chest, providing the fan with a nice memento of the occasion. Who of the two displayed the poorer judgment in that case? You make the call on that one.

Seven years later, the Indians faced the New York Yankees in the American League Championship Series. An ugly scene emerged before the fifth game even started, as the Yankees' starter David Wells was warming up before the game. A handful of fans began yelling at the pitcher, and then it turned really ugly. They started to taunt him over the fact of his mother's recent death. Perhaps the Indians' fans had become crazed after having watched the team drop the seventh game of the previous year's series, but there was no excuse for that kind of behavior.

What made it even more embarrassing, as he would recount a few years later in an interview in the *Chicago Sun-Times*, was the handful of fans turned into "like

The next time a Cleveland sports team wins a championship, I will . . .
"have already been dead from a heart attack that they got that far, so I'll come back from the dead to dance in the streets." — Laura Gump, Akron

chapter 3: poor judgment

Browns fans go to great length to show their support. Loyal fans seem willing to risk even pneumonia to show their diehard spirit. *(Ron Kuntz photo)*

50 or 60 people, and it got contagious, like cancer spreading. Everyone got in on the act."

These highlighted moments don't include hosts of other displays of poor judgment that never made the headlines.

Dan Maust of North Olmsted remembers a game in the early 1990s when he was sitting in the upper benches of the Dawg Pound. He happened to look back at a guy in the last row of the Dawg Pound - the row closest to the huge, hulking scoreboard that loomed over the Pound.

"This guy's drinking out of a thermos, finishes it, and just heaves it into the middle of the crowd," said Maust.

If that wasn't bad enough, Jeff Richman of Highland Heights, another fan, remembers sitting in Cleveland Municipal Stadium at Indians' games and looking up at the upper deck sections behind left center field and left field. His lasting memories: "A lot of people used to have sex in the seats near the rafters," Richman said.

Browns' fans who attended games at old Municipal Stadium remember the ridiculously long lines for the bathrooms. In the men's rooms, the stories were endless about the ways fans found to relieve themselves. The most common place to take care of business, when the long, metal troughs were too crowded, was against the restroom walls. If wall space was taken up, then into the sink you went. When you have to go, you go.

John Thompson, a.k.a. Big Dawg, recalled numerous instances of attention-grabbing behavior. During the heyday of the Dawg Pound, a Steelers' fan walked into the bleacher section wearing black and gold and yelling, "Screw the Browns!"

surviving the drought: cleveland sports fans since 1964

It's not easy to juggle a beer and at the same time show Quincy Morgan, who just scored a touchdown, some serious love. Dawg Pound fans are known for their passionate enthusiasm, if not always their best judgment. *(Ron Kuntz photo)*

"The guy walked into a hornets' nest - it was incredible," Thompson said in an interview. Within minutes, fans stripped him down to his underwear and burned his clothes right in front of him.

Another time, an usher who was assigned near the Dawg Pound tried to calm down some of the activity in a section of the bleachers.

"He starts pointing at guys and telling them they're going to be thrown out for drinking, and the guys near the keg in the dog house instantly stood up and beer-washed this guy," he said. "The usher probably had 30-40 cups of beer hit him at the same time."

In *Legends by the Lake*, Thompson recalled that in 1995 he and other Dawg Pound fans built a bonfire using garb ripped directly off Steelers' fans - like coats, towels, and other apparel. As he remembered, "we were burning them to keep warm and roast weenies."

So it has happened that passion has occasionally slipped into foolhardiness, and frustrations have been expressed by rowdiness. As a result, Cleveland fans have earned the reputation of being passionate to a fault - to a point of being downright unruly. As Al Lerner said after the 2001 Jacksonville game, some Cleveland fans have become known as "not the most stable."

Then again, most Clevelanders have always sort of known that. The line between fervor and foolishness is easily blurred, especially after a few beers.

4 next year
surviving the drought

"Let me tell you something, my friend. Hope is a dangerous thing. Hope can drive a man insane." — Red, *The Shawshank Redemption*

Quick. Name the most common phrase to jump from the mouths of Cleveland sports fans.

"Next year." More than any other words - of course, not counting the colorful four-letter variety of obscenities - these two words are a staple of Cleveland fans' verbal diet. Whenever they are starved for conversation, they can simply utter those simple words, and they will get their fill. Once infused with this phrase, awkward, stumbling small talk on the Shaker Rapid can convert complete strangers into veritable blood brothers of hope.

Although much of the movie *Shawshank Redemption* was filmed just outside Cleveland -in Mansfield, to be precise - you'd think it was filmed right in the heart of the city. Take a look at Cleveland sports fans, and you'll see that the hope Cleveland fans have been desperately clinging to every year for the last 43 has probably turned a fair number psychologically impaired.

We insanely utter "next year" faster than the Waco Kid could draw a loaded gun. The Browns just gave up the touchdown in the Dawg Pound end of the AFC Championship game with just over a minute left? "Next year." Michael Jordan just reached down our windpipes and ripped out our lungs with a buzzer-beating shot? "Next year." Craig Counsell zips across home plate in Miami to send the Indians back to Ohio as the American League - not the World Series - champs? "Next year." Ugh.

But of the three Cleveland major league teams during the past 43 years, probably more people pinned their hopes on the Browns as the Cleveland team most likely to reach the promised land the

surviving the drought: cleveland sports fans since 1964

In January, the Browns' season over and the Indians' season still three months away, with snow covering the city and the old Cleveland Stadium, fans always seem to renew their hope and think about "next year." *(Ron Kuntz photo)*

following year. Many Clevelanders actually believed the upcoming year would produce a Super Bowl trip

Sadly, the Cleveland Browns, once one of the winningest teams in NFL history, is one of only five teams never to even make it to the Super Bowl. And we're not talking about getting tickets for good seats, either.

Yet, how many times has a Browns' squad come tantalizingly close to the big show? Look at the 1960s. Year after year, the Browns almost made the championship game, which became known as the Super Bowl in 1967. Cleveland fans awaited each new season with high expectation that come January they would be glued to their seats as their Browns would battle for the title. Then, for most of the 1970s, the Browns took a hiatus from real competitiveness, save periodically for some intense games against the mighty Steelers.

During that same time, the Tribe would leave its spring training home in Arizona and get lost somewhere between the desert and the southern shore of Lake Erie. The Cavs were just starting as an NBA expansion team; there were few expectations there.

When the 1980s arrived, "next year" took on a more desperate tone, courtesy of the gut-wrenching, heart-pounding finishes of the 1980 Kardiac Kids. It's as if the Kardiac Kids awakened what many have referred to as the "sleeping giant" - the mass of intensely passionate Cleveland sports fans - and gave them a taste of respect they hadn't had in years.

In subsequent seasons throughout the 1980s, Clevelanders' great expectations were encouraged even by outsiders who thought the Browns might have what it

chapter 4: next year

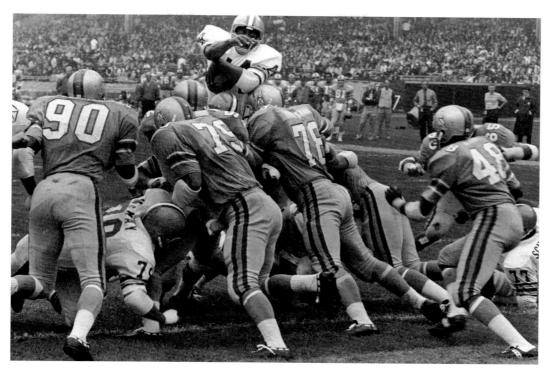

After Leroy Kelly led the Browns to a 1971 season-opening 31-0 victory over the Houston Oilers, hopes soared for Cleveland fans. Maybe this would be the year, they hoped. After a mid-season slump, the Browns put together five straight victories to end the regular season. They then were thumped by the Baltimore Colts, 20-3, in the first playoff game. *(Mitchael Zaremba photo, Cleveland Public Library collection)*

took to make it to the Super Bowl. Take the 1984 season, for example. That year, *Playboy* predicted that the Browns would win the AFC and meet the San Francisco 49ers in the big show. As usual with major predictions when Cleveland teams were part of the mix, the experts got half of it right - the half that wasn't the Cleveland team. Unfortunately, besides an excellent defense that featured some of the top linebackers in the game (Chip Banks, Tom Cousineau, Clay Matthews, and Dick Ambrose), the Browns heading into the 1984 season lacked basically everything else needed for a successful run at the Super Bowl.

The pass rush didn't exist. The starting quarterback - Paul McDonald - hadn't been able to beat out Brian Sipe for two years and sported the league's worst quarterback rating in 1983. And head coach Sam Rutigliano kept publicly reminding Clevelanders and the front office that it would be nice to have some speed at wide receiver (apparently Ricky Feacher and Willie Adams weren't the answer).

But even Rutigliano's glass seemed half full. He predicted the Browns would capture the AFC Central Division crown. In an interview, he admitted that telling Clevelanders to have patience wasn't an incredibly popular thing to do. He called it "verbal diarrhea." He probably thought of that phrase while listening to Art Modell's comments to the press week after week.

Of the other prognosticators, most believed the Browns too imbalanced to do much damage that year. Paul Zimmerman of *Sports Illustrated* and Howard Balzer of *The Sporting News* predicted the Browns would finish third in the four-team division, just ahead of Houston. Balzer did acknowledge the role of hope in reference

surviving the drought: cleveland sports fans since 1964

Opening Day for the 1970 baseball season at Cleveland Stadium had almost as many people on the field as in the stands. The 1969 team had been predicted to go all the way, but instead finished 62-99. In April 1970, the fans were not yet ready to again let their hopes climb too high.
(Richard Conway photo, Cleveland Public Library collection)

to McDonald. He said the Browns had been "blowing a lot of smoke his way, but it's been fueled mostly by hope."

Welcome to Cleveland, Howard.

When the season started, if there had been any diarrhea going around, it seemed to take hold of the brown and orange. Eight weeks into the season the Browns sported a 1-7 record and Art Modell asked Rutigliano - who a few weeks earlier had said he was "good for the City of Cleveland" and that Cleveland fans were "lucky that I'm here" - to take his luck elsewhere. The team finished 5-11 under Marty Schottenheimer.

In 1985, the arrival of the young University of Miami star Bernie Kosar fueled more optimism. The Browns that year took a ho-hum 8-8 record into the playoffs, looked up at the scoreboard in the 3rd quarter of their playoff game against the Dolphins in Miami, noticed they were ahead 21-3 after a 66-yard scamper by Ernest Byner, and then lost the game, 24-21.

Throw more kindling onto the flames of hope: 1986 meant a maturing Kosar, proven running backs, and a solid defense.

And so the hope-filled years of subsequent Browns' history began with more predictions: *Sports Illustrated* en-

The next time a Cleveland sports team wins a championship, I will . . .

"appreciate the moment for my children, who will really enjoy it, because the first game I ever covered for the Browns was the 1964 championship game," — Dan Coughlin

chapter 4: next year

Amid the many unhappy moments Cleveland Browns' fans have had to endure against the Pittsburgh Steelers, there are some more cheerful moments. Joe Jones' head-rattling sack of Terry Bradshaw was one such moment. *(Paul Tepley photo)*

visioned the Browns making the Super Bowl in 1986, and when they lost to Denver, foresaw a Browns' Super Bowl journey for the 1987 season. The New York *Times* opined in September 1987 that the Browns and the Patriots were the favorites to represent the AFC in the Super Bowl. At the start of the 1988 campaign, after the Browns had lost to John Elway and the Broncos a second straight year in the AFC Championship game, The *Sporting News* commented that the Browns were "confident they can get over the hump this year . . . they have enough playoff experience now that there should be no fear of cracking under pressure." Vegas odds in 1988 favored the Browns to win the crown (4-1 favorites), ahead of Denver (6-1) and the New York Giants (6-1).

In those heady years, how many times Browns' fans opened their newspapers or sports magazines and read something on the cover like The *Sporting News* football preview of 1988: "Is this the year Bernie does it for the Browns?"

Everyone now knows the answer was no, but we still love to read those pieces and can barely contain our excitement when a major magazine chooses a Cleveland team or player to highlight. Any bit of hope is like a life raft in a sea of drowning sports sorrows.

In a piece by The *Sporting News*' Jeff Schudel titled "Great Expectations," in which he spotlighted Kosar, he reminded football fans that Kosar was six the last time the Browns had won a playoff game (1969 against Dallas), and the Browns had remained winless in the post-season until the gangly-legged wonder boy led Cleveland past the Jets in the double-overtime thriller against the New York Jets in January 1987.

Vinny Testaverde, who became the Browns starting quarterback in 1993 after Bernie Kosar was demoted, signals "touchdown" as running back Tommy Vardell crosses the goal line in a 1994 pre-season game against the Atlanta Falcons. The Browns' trip to the playoffs that season renewed talk of a Cleveland trip to the Super Bowl in 1995.
(Cleveland Browns photo, Cleveland Landmarks Press Collection)

The ultimate unfolding of what actually took place in those seasons is almost too hard to describe. Look at the outcomes during those exciting years:

SEASON	FINAL GAME	OPPONENTS	OUTCOME
1985	Division Playoff	Miami plays Browns in Miami	Browns lose, 24-21
1986	AFC Championship	Denver plays Browns in Cleveland	Browns lose, 23-20, OT
1987	AFC Championship	Denver plays Browns in Denver	Browns lose, 38-33
1988	Division Playoff	Houston plays Browns in Cleveland	Browns lose, 24-23
1989	AFC Championship	Denver plays Browns in Denver	Browns lose, 37-21

By 1988, the headlines smacked of pity. Yet Cleveland fans still loved to read those pieces and could barely contain their excitement that someone liked us, even if the predictions were like Paul Zimmerman's of *Sports Illustrated*. He put it bluntly: "Here's why everyone is picking the Cleveland Browns to go the Super Bowl: People are tired of Denver."

Not exactly a rousing endorsement, but Cleveland fans couldn't hide the wide smiles that emerged on their mugs after reading it. At least their pain and suffering were recognized by fans elsewhere, and that was some consolation. Not much, but some.

Looking on the bright side, after the 1989 season the Browns weren't predicted

chapter 4: next year

Matt Stover tries for a field goal against the Houston Oilers during a snowy November game at Municipal Stadium in 1994. Mark Rypien is the holder.
(Cleveland Browns photo, Cleveland Landmarks Press collection)

by local or national media to do much. What bright side? Well, Cleveland fans didn't have the almost unbearable - especially after such miserable outcomes year after year in the 1980s - burden of carrying hope around from the next training camp until January. That load can get heavy. And depressing.

Enter the 1994 season, a new coach (Bill Belicheck), a new quarterback (Todd Philcox - no, Vinny Testaverde), new personnel all over the offense and defense, an eventual playoff victory against the New England Patriots, and a playoff loss to the Pittsburgh Steelers, and . . . you know where this story is going.

In summer 1995, while the Tribe rolled over opponents and while debates raged about the future of the Browns and Modell's frustrations about negotiations over a stadium deal, the Browns promptly filled some holes in their team that convinced some that 1995 was the Browns' year. For what? Well, we know that 1995 turned out to be the Browns' year to shake Cleveland fans to the core - but not in ecstasy over a Super Bowl trip.

Paul Zimmerman of *Sports Illustrated* explained why he thought the Browns would represent the AFC in Super Bowl XXX. He called it the "anger factor." The Browns had lost three times in 1994 to the Steelers, and he argued that the final loss - a 29-9 playoff drubbing in Pittsburgh - left the Brownies steaming and "ready to resume the argument."

That off-season, the Browns added Andre Rison, who would turn out to be about as popular in Cleveland as, well, Bill Belicheck was at the time. With quarterback Eric Zeier, who Zimmerman said had "that certain something that the great ones have," and Ernest Hunter (who?), a halfback out of NAIA, the Browns, he

surviving the drought: cleveland sports fans since 1964

Tony Martinez and Rocky Colavito greet Max Alvis as he crosses home plate in 1965. It was Colavito's first year back after General Manager Frank Lane traded him to Detroit for the 1960 season, probably the most unpopular trade in Indians' history. The year Rocky was traded attendance fell by over 540,000; the year he returned it climbed by 280,000. Cleveland fans are not to be toyed with. *(Cleveland Public Library collection)*

said, had put the finishing touches on a Super Bowl roster. We all know how that year really ended.

Unfortunately - or maybe fortunately because they did not raise false hopes for Cleveland fans - predictions of first-place finishes or even for serious playoff contention for the Indians hit some serious dry spells over the last 43 years. In the 1960s, for instance, writers polled fans and listed their responses alongside the experts' forecasts. Chiefly they regarded the Indians as having relatively solid clubs some years, and in other years squads that really didn't merit much attention.

The pre-season prediction lists for the Tribe in the late 1960s are probably not unlike tea parties - warmly pleasant, but surely not quite fulfilling. Of course, for die-hard Cleveland fans, the predictions also probably left them feeling like they had just taken a bite of someone else's tea biscuit - blah. In 1965, The *Sporting News* baseball writers and fans predicted a fourth-place finish out of the ten American League teams. Apparently the heralded return of slugger Rocky Colavito wasn't enough to boost prospects. The next year brought a ho-hum fifth place prediction, even if Russell Schneider, The *Plain Dealer*

The next time a Cleveland sports team wins a championship, I will . . .

"definitely enjoy it to its fullest, and not say anything about repeating the next year. And definitely not say this is the start of a dynasty," — Jim Donovan

chapter 4: next year

Luis Tiant's brilliant year on the mound for the Tribe in 1968 helped that squad have its best record in years. In one game that year he fanned 19 batters, the Indians' all-time record.
(Cleveland Press Collection of the Cleveland State University Libraries)

reporter and regular Indians contributor to The *Sporting News*, meekly wrote that the team was good enough to win the pennant. They eventually finished 81-81.

In 1968, which actually turned out to be a better year for the Cleveland nine than most, experts and fans predicted them to finish in seventh place. The squad eventually racked up 86 victories, helped in large part by Luis Tiant's 21-9 record and 1.60 ERA, and their third-place finish encouraged many to think that 1969 might bring a pennant run. The team in 1969, however, went 62-99, despite being widely expected to bring home a pennant for the first time in more than a decade.

The Indians' bats, and their gloves, and their arms, and - you get the picture - continued to sleep for a good portion of the 1970s and 1980s. It defies logic how a new group of players, year in and year out, could produce such staggeringly similar results. And yet, just when Cleveland fans might have given up hope, just when Cleveland fans were ready finally to write off the Indians to Tampa Bay (the rumors emerged, week after week, that the Indians would be shipped south to a place that would draw more than 10,000 fans per game) enter the 1986 Cleveland Indians.

Following a miserable - and typical - season in 1985 in which the Tribe finished in last place in the American League East and dropped 105 games, the 1986 Indians seemed to have a raw energy, if nothing else.

What a fun team to watch. The offense led the league in hitting and scoring behind the bats of Cory Snyder, Joe Carter, Pat Tabler, Brook Jacoby, Julio Franco, Brett Butler, Mel Hall, and Tony Bernazard. The pitching was mediocre, but had enough gas until August, when the

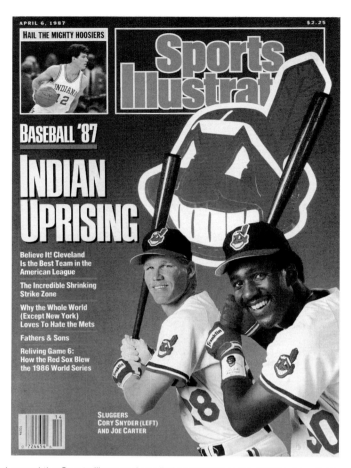

Most sports fans who read the Sports Illustrated prediction probably said, "Come on – the team from Cleveland? The baseball team? Really?" Well, no, it turned out. *(Lane Stewart photo, Sports Illustrated)*

Indians started to slide. That was impressive enough. For Cleveland Indians fans, the season was typically shot by the All-Star break.

Greg Swindell, after getting trounced by Boston in his debut, settled down. Tom Candiotti posted 16 victories, Ken Schrom was 14-7, Scott Bailes finished 10-10, and even 47-year old Phil Neikro contributed 11 wins. Throw in some impressive winning streaks - like a 10-game streak in April and May, and a seven-gamer in July - and a Pat Corrales karate kick to Oakland A's pitcher Dave Stewart, and the fans came out in droves. Their attendance in 1986 (1,471,805) looked like a misprint, when one compared it to that of 1985 (655,181).

They finished 84-78, above .500 for the first time in five years and 11 $\frac{1}{2}$ games out of first, the closest they had come to winning the AL East since 1981.

As April rolled around and the prognosticators revved up their engines, *Sports Illustrated* had the audacity to put Carter and Snyder on the cover and call them the best team in the American League. That's right - they picked the explosive club to capture the pennant for the first time since 1954. The *New York Times* predicted they would finish second to Toronto. These were giddy predictions for a club that was typically out of the race in June.

And there was more - many managers and players also seemed to think 1987 was the Tribe's year. Cincinnati Reds' Manager

chapter 4: next year

In 1993, the Indians played their last season at Cleveland Municipal Stadium. The final game there, October 3, 1993, was a sellout. The Indians ended the season in sixth place. Fans that day must have been hoping that their investment in new facilities for both the Indians and the Cavaliers at Gateway would result in happier days. *(David Kachinko photo)*

Pete Rose boldly proclaimed that it was the Indians' turn to win the division, because for the previous six years, a different team had captured the AL East title each year.

"How many teams are in the division? Seven? . . . That's kind of strange a far as I'm concerned. Everybody's won it but the Indians. It's their turn," Rose said.

OK - not exactly a prediction based on who was taking the field, but still, the guy knew baseball, didn't he? Maybe the fact that Rose predicted the Tribe to win it should have been a warning sign. The guy soon was kicked out of baseball for betting on the game as a manager, and is still not eligible for Cooperstown.

Even Bob Feller jumped on the "I-haven't-learned-a-thing-about-predicting-a-Cleveland-championship" bandwagon by comparing the 1987 club to the 1948 squad.

"We didn't have great pitchers in '48," he said.

Perhaps. But did the 1948 World Series Champions sport the likes of Rich Yett, Ed VandeBerg, Ernie Camacho, Chris Codorili, Tom Waddell, Jeff Dedmon, and the rest of what would become known as the "Bullpen from Hell?" Sure, the 1987 Tribe could boast two veterans on the pitching staff (Niekro and late spring acquisition Steve Carlton), but their combined age probably exceeded Forest Gump's IQ.

In Cleveland, though, reporters were less enthusiastic, albeit still hopeful. Bill Livingston predicted that the pennant still looked a year off, and Gene Williams thought the Tribe would likely finish third, in preparation for a serious run in 1988. Of the three reporters who predicted the winners of the 1987 baseball campaign, Livingston and Williams forecasted a

Nate Thurmond drives for the basket. Nate the Great was nearing the end of his career when he was traded to the Cavs, but he came in time to be a part of the exciting "Miracle of Richfield" year.
(Cleveland Press *Collection of the Cleveland State University Libraries)*

third-place finish, and the Indians' regular beat reporter, Paul Hoynes, picked them to finish fourth.

The script as it actually played out became an all too familiar drama. Perhaps we might call it a tragedy? Or was it a comedy? The Tribe posted 101 losses and finished dead last. The team was dead wood. Players seemed dead as door nails. They played like Dead Heads.

For the next few years, few people expected much from the Tribe. In 1989 they posted another 100-loss season and began to trade the remaining marketable talent to other, contending teams. Same old story, right?

Wrong, it turned out. Joe Carter was shipped to San Diego for Sandy Alomar, Jr., and Carlos Baerga in 1989. Eddie Taubense and Willie Blair were sent packing for Houston to welcome Kenny Lofton in 1991. Tom Candiotti was allowed to go to the Los Angeles Dodgers in 1992 to free up money. The Indians, unbeknownst to many baseball fans, were positioning themselves for a run at glory.

At the end of the 1993 season, as the Tribe finished its days as a tenant in old Cleveland Municipal Stadium, many people felt hopeful. Although tragedy had struck the team to start the 1993 season with the deaths of teammates Steve Olin and Tim Crews, the Tribe posted a 76-86 record for the second straight year. The important story, besides the efforts by the players and management to overcome

The next time a Cleveland sports team wins a championship, I will . . .
"say my life is complete," — Bill Fritz, Mogadore

chapter 4: next year

The ball gets away from forward Campy Russell who was a dependable shot maker.
Russell is currently part of the Cavs' television broadcast team.
(Cleveland Press *Collection of the Cleveland State University Libraries)*

the grief from the spring training accident, was the club's budding talent. On the roster besides Lofton, Baerga, and Alomar, Jr., were Paul Sorrento, Jim Thome, Manny Ramirez, and Albert Belle. Add off-season acquisitions Eddie Murray, Omar Vizquel (in a trade of Felix Fermin - how about that one?), Dennis Martinez, and cap it off with a new ballpark called Jacobs Field, and the stage was set for something special.

The strike-shortened season of 1994 was a brutal blow to Tribe fans, since for the first time in decades, predictions for the Indians were that they would make a run at the American League Central Division title. Amazingly, in August, when the season was stopped, the Tribe found itself at 66-47, one game behind the powerful Chicago White Sox, who experts had predicted would win the division.

So the Tribe was predicted to be good, and it actually was good. What a recipe for head-in-the-clouds excitement. Throw in a dash of veteran help (Orel Hershiser, Dave Winfield, and Tony Pena), a splattering of Browns' disappointment and controversy (Bernie Kosar was ignominiously dropped midway through the 1993 season, Belicheck was putting people to sleep in press conferences, Modell was saying he wouldn't hire another coach . . . blah, blah, blah), and so in 1995 fans pinned their hopes on the Indians. It was a great year, but ultimately Atlanta went home with the big prize.

What about the predictions for the Cavs over the last three-plus decades? Knowing how poor to mediocre they were for the first 15 years of the club's existence - except for the Miracle of Richfield in 1976 - it's understandable that no one really predicted them to compete for postseason play.

Zydrunas Ilgauskas, like Cleveland fans, has had to look forward to the next year more than once as foot injuries cost him nearly four seasons. But like the fans, "Z" did not give up and has become the Cavalier's longest-tenured player. *(Karin McKenna photo)*

Then, in 1986, the Cavaliers began to reverse a fairly pathetic draft history of early round picks that never amounted to much. From 1979-1985, only three players were chosen in the first three rounds who eventually became NBA stars. Bill Laimbeer was selected in the third round in 1979, but he would be dealt three years later. Cleveland native Charles Oakley, who was chosen in the first round in 1985, was then immediately traded to New York for two busts (Keith Lee and Ennis Whatley). John "Hot Rod" Williams, a second-round pick in 1985, was a keeper.

In 1986, the Cavs scored huge returns when they selected Brad Daugherty and Ron Harper in the first round. Then they pulled off a trade to acquire the Mavericks' second-round pick, Mark Price. As a side note, Cavs' fans probably remember that the team selected Daugherty as the first overall pick amidst a chorus of boos and criticisms from the local and national media and fans, most of whom expected the team to choose the supposed best player, Len Bias. But this time the choice was right, for Bias, within 48 hours of being selected by the Boston Celtics as the number two pick, died of heart complications brought on by cocaine.

Prognostications of competitiveness for the Cavaliers during this era didn't really emerge until after the team acquired Mike Sanders and Larry Nance in the middle of the 1987-1988 season, in which the team would finish with a 42-40 record and lose to Michael Jordan and the Bulls in the opening playoff round.

Heading into the 1988-1989 season, *Sports Illustrated* predicted that the team, which they said was "without a star," could make a serious run for a conference championship despite its youth. The *Plain Dealer* predicted a second-place finish,

chapter 4: next year

This young fan's sign tells the story of most Indians' rooters. It also reveals the ever-changing nature of the team roster, as Tribe management tries to put together all the pieces. One year after this 2006 shot was taken, four of the named players had moved on to other teams. *(Ron Kuntz photo)*

noting that the outlook was the best since 1976. The Cavs, of course, did make a run and set a franchise record for wins (57), but then lost to the Bulls again - this time a result of "The Shot."

Between 1989-1992, probably the longest run of talent for the Cavs in franchise history, experts basically suggested that while the team was excellent, they questioned whether it could get past the other three dominant teams at the time - Atlanta, Chicago, and Detroit. Partly due to recurring injuries to Daugherty, Price, and Nance, and partly because, as *Sports Illustrated* said in 1990, they didn't have enough "fire-in-the-belly" players to beat the elite teams, the Cavs were regularly regarded as the third- or fourth-best team in the conference. Even in 1992, after the team acquired star Gerald Wilkins, *Sports Illustrated* opined that there was still something missing from the team,

like "Toughness. True hunger. Nastiness. An us-against-the-world, we'll-show-'em mentality."

The *Plain Dealer* sports writers (Burt Graeff, Bob Dolgan, Bill Livingston, and Bud Shaw) were a bit more positive, predicting the team would get to the Eastern Conference finals before bowing to the Bulls. For a truly heartwarming prediction, oddly enough one had to go to New York. The New York *Times*' Harvey Araton forecast the Cavs as NBA champs. This time, though, the Cleveland sports writers were dead on, as the Cavs would fall to the Bulls in six games in the Eastern Conference finals.

So what is the moral of the story? Who knows? Probably Cleveland fans can think of a bunch of adages: "the more things change, the more they stay the same"; "Life is like a box of chocolates: you never know what you're going to

Cleveland fans continue to root ardently for their teams. Here four young fans show their support for popular center fielder Grady Sizemore. Not old enough to remember the many years of championship frustration, they hope Sizemore will lead the team to the ultimate goal. *(Ron Kuntz photos)*

get"; "Don't count your chickens before they're hatched"; "Take time to stop and smell the roses." Being a Cleveland sports fan requires painful exercises in finding hope amid heartbreak.

Perhaps you're thinking the moral of the story is that sports writers and prognosticators know about as much as ordinary fans do. Or perhaps you're concluding that the relationship between predictions of major sports gurus and ultimate success of Cleveland teams is in inverse proportion; the more the pros think Cleveland teams will succeed, the more they don't. Of course, that's not a perfect relationship either. It seems that when the experts predict Cleveland teams not to win, they typically are right on the money.

Maybe Cleveland fans will swear off hope and remember the words of Red from *The Shawshank Redemption* - that hope can drive a person insane. Then again, there is next year, and a little positive thinking never hurt anyone. Right?

5 Surviving the drought
inner lives of cleveland fans

Most men live lives of quiet desperation. — Henry David Thoreau

The stories are endless. Walk around Greater Cleveland and just find out. Since 1964, Cleveland fans have trials and tribulations that are more powerful, moving, and often, ultimately more tragic than any fan base in the country.

Who are the legions who claim loyalty to the regularly mediocre and often bad Cleveland teams that have taken the courts or the fields in the last 43 years? What kind of person seems to take pride in his or her devotion to utterly forgettable athletes and squads? Are they distinctly different from the faithful followers of other major cities?

Spend some time in Greater Cleveland, and the answer is clear. Cleveland sports devotees are a unique bunch. Hands down.

The people who live and die for the Browns, Indians, and Cavs - largely because they have wandered the desert for more than 43 years hoping for a quenching gulp from the championship spring - are in no small measure passionate, desperate, loyal, and hopeful.

How does one know? Talk to them.

Charlie Price, who grew up in Mayfield in the 1970s and 80s, remembers when the passion brought about an explosive conclusion. He was at a party for the AFC Championship of the 1987 season - when the Browns played the Broncos in Denver. During the first half, when the Browns were abused and looked clueless, one fan at the party kept loudly saying over and over again, "The Browns suck!" The Browns, after all, were down 21-3 at the half. At the start of the second half, Kosar and the Browns' offense were resuscitated. Play by play, yard by yard, minute by minute, the Browns made it a game. As football fans know, the Browns

surviving the drought: cleveland sports fans since 1964

During the 1970s Browns' fans did not have much to cheer about, and particularly galling was their 5-15 record against arch-rival Pittsburgh Steelers. Here Mack Mitchell and Jerry Sherk try in vain to stop a Terry Bradshaw pass. *(Cleveland Browns photo, Cleveland Landmarks Press collection)*

reached within one touchdown and were driving in the final minutes to tie the score. At that point, the fan who in the first half had been proclaiming his opinion about the Browns as if it were theological truth was beyond himself, out-of-control, cheering on the team he had so recently reviled. The phrase hadn't been uttered in a while.

Then, The Fumble.

An instance of silence. An instance of disbelief.

The fan who had uttered the desperate three-word phrase throughout the first half broke that silence with that same, stinging, brutal phrase.

"The Browns suck!"

Instantly, a big man at the party, actually a huge man, stood up, red-faced and provoked.

"Get out! Get out of my house!" he screamed. People looked around awkwardly. "I mean it! Get out!" The partygoers sheepishly got up and filed out of the house.

What makes the story pathetic was the fact that it was a party for high school kids. The fan disparaging the Browns in the first half was a 16-year-old, and the guy who demanded they leave was the fa-

The next time a Cleveland sports team wins a championship, I will . . .
"make sure the nation hears me say, "wait until next year, when we go back to back," — Brian Cayne, University Heights

chapter 5: inner lives

The baby instinctively knows there has been so much to cry about. Unfortunately, Tribe outfield Mel Hall bore the brunt of this crying fit. *(Ron Kuntz photo)*

ther of one of the teenagers. That's right. The passion that Cleveland sports unleash can even destabilize adults.

Sometimes the fans are almost incomprehensibly passionate in their enthusiasm. One can always tell Cleveland fans in a crowd. They're shrieking louder than everyone else. They're the ones talking excitedly and nonstop, as if somehow to distract themselves from, well, themselves. And in truth, the team doesn't even have to be real - they are the same people who go nuts watching the 1989 movie *Major League,* a film about a (fairly typical for that era) team of lovable losers dressed in Cleveland Indians' uniforms who turned it around to win the pennant. A work of fiction? No matter. Seen it a hundred times? No matter. They still go bonkers because not only can they share in a moment of pure sports bliss, but they can actually be proud that the movie is about a *Cleveland* team – even though aggravatingly most of it was filmed in Milwaukee instead of Cleveland.

For the last 43 years, there have been many times when Cleveland teams have been good enough to draw people into a world of desperate fanaticism. Even when the squads were ho-hum, like the Browns in the 1970s, they would sometimes play the mighty Pittsburgh Steelers as if they belonged on the same field. Same goes in baseball. Even when the Tribe turned out disappointingly ordinary seasons, they could play well against the powerhouses, like the New York Yankees.

And when Cleveland teams showed even a glimpse of competitiveness, the fans came out in droves. In 1986, the Indians, for the first time since many Clevelanders could remember, played exciting baseball and had a crop of young stars. They would eventually finish in

surviving the drought: cleveland sports fans since 1964

Cleveland fans are sturdy souls. A few snowflakes are unlikely to deter them from showing up for a football game-or even lining up outside Jacobs Field to see a "springtime" Indians' game. *(Ron Kuntz photo)*

fifth place and above .500 (84-78) for only the fourth time in 18 years. Compared to years past, fans tripped over each other to get to games - one drew more than 61,000, and one in June brought more than 73,000. Granted, they were encouraged by promotions, but when was the last time someone heard of those numbers turning out for baseball? In total, the 1986 campaign brought out more than 1.4 million fans - a number that had not been seen since 1959.

WJW's Dan Coughlin remembers the 1986 season fondly. Its most striking element was the simple fact that the organization seemed unprepared for even a little success.

"In May, the Tribe came home with a 10-game winning streak. They didn't have enough ticket takers when the gates opened, so the crowd couldn't get in, even though it was a crowd of only 35,000," he said.

Sure, one could point to the time between, say, 1960 and 1985 and wonder why the average attendance at Tribe games was in the neighborhood of 10,000, and sometimes fewer. And because of those numbers an outsider might challenge the assertion that Cleveland sports fans are an exceptionally passionate, loyal bunch. But one must understand that during those 25 years, for instance, Cleveland fans who did come through the turnstiles didn't really see anyone on the diamond. It was like in the *Field of Dreams* - they sat in the stands but couldn't see any real baseball players. Yet because it had been built (and Cleveland Municipal Stadium had been there since 1931, so it wasn't exactly state-of-the-art), they came, hoping that somehow players as good as Shoeless Joe would materialize before their very eyes. Actually, taking this into account, one might be impressed by the

chapter 5: inner lives

Cleveland fans enjoyed the fact that the Cleveland Indians were the subject of the 1989 comedy *Major League*, about a group of misfits turned pennant contenders. Tom Berenger and Charlie Sheen starred in the movie, some of which was filmed in Cleveland Municipal Stadium. *(Janet Macoska photo, Western Reserve Historical Society collection)*

numbers that did turn out during that time to watch *nothing*.

Think about it: in the 25 years between 1969-1993, the Indians finished better than .500 exactly four times. Many people in the Cleveland area were born, lived, and died during that stretch. And even though you may be blessed with a considerably longer lifespan, you may never see a championship, either, so don't go feeling too sorry for them.

In recent years, Jacobs Field, even after the 455 consecutive sold-out game streak ended in 2001, still draws on average more than 25,000 even though the baseball team has taken a relative talent dive from the heady days of the 1990s.

With regard to football, Clevelanders still regularly sell out Cleveland Browns Stadium. This cannot be overstated. The heyday of Browns competitiveness ebbed in the 1960s, then took a dive through most of the 1970s and into the mid-1980s. During that time, sellouts were still common. Tailgating in the parking lots near the Stadium was constant. The Muny and Port lots were always whirlwinds of shouting, drinking, frivolity, music, and laughter. Even during those times of mediocre play and although the skies were gray and the winds howled in from white-capped Lake Erie, fans tailgated every Sunday and commiserated with each other. Notwithstanding Art Modell's

surviving the drought: cleveland sports fans since 1964

Cleveland has been sometimes called the "sleeping giant." The belief is that the fans have been waiting to be awoken and will turn out in record numbers to watch competitive teams. But even in the bad old days of the Indians' last four decades at the old Stadium, there were occasions that fans would fill the place. The roar of the 70,000 plus crowd on those days could not be beat. *(Janet Macosko photo, Western Reserve Historical Society collection)*

1995 claims of financial disaster and nonsupport, even when the Browns hit rock bottom in the early 1990s after several years of playoff contention, fans were still paying to see the team play.

Consider their most recent odyssey through the desert. Since the franchise returned in 1999, the Browns have churned out a miserable 40-88 record. One of those eight seasons miraculously produced a trip to the playoffs, before the losing set in again. How have fans responded? With sellouts, of course.

Terry Pluto, the award-winning writer for The *Plain Dealer* who has covered Cleveland sports for years, said the most amazing sight he ever beheld regarding Cleveland fans' passionate loyalty happened just after Modell announced the Browns' move. Enraged over the thought of losing their beloved Browns, the fans still turned out for the last games of that horrific 1995 season.

"It was the most incredible thing - to see 55,000-60,000 fans showing up after the move was announced," Pluto said. "It was mind boggling."

So let's review: put nobody on a baseball diamond (and in a decrepit old stadium), and 10,000 fans show up every night. Tell everyone you're uprooting the team from Cleveland, and sell about 80% of your tickets. Make a competitive run for a few seasons, and watch as Cleve-

The next time a Cleveland sports team wins a championship, I will . . .
"be there celebrating in the streets and watching as Cleveland fans tear the city apart," — Linda Lewis, Akron

chapter 5: inner lives

For many years in the old stadium, Abe Abraham, in his brown suit, gave devoted service, standing outside the end zone to catch field goals, a part of the rich Browns' tradition. Abe is gone, and so is the old Stadium. Fans are still waiting for the magic to appear in the new one. *(Charles Proctor photo, Western Reserve Historical Society)*

landers sell out the season before it even begins. Season after season. All this goes to prove is that if a professional team in Cleveland is competitive, the fans fit their fannies into the seats. It's that simple.

It has been a bit different with regard to the Cavs, who entered the NBA as an expansion franchise in 1970. Because the team has not had as long a history as the other two teams, and because, in the short history that it has had, it has only had glimpses of real competitiveness, the Cavs have been the third most popular team in Cleveland.

But consider that since the Cavs have improved their records from their dismal 17-win 2002-3 campaign and completed two consecutive 50-win seasons, Cleveland fans have responded in droves. They set a franchise record for average game attendance (20,437) in the 2006-7 season, breaking its previous home attendance record of 20,338 set in 1994-95. They set a franchise record for the most sellouts at the Q (32 out of 41), and drew the league's third highest home attendance. With LeBron James and a bright future he brings, the Cavs personify the hope that the Northeast Ohio faithful clings to.

The passion that Cleveland fans exhibit often makes them look like a feisty bunch, too. Soon after Art Modell announced the Browns out of Cleveland, hundreds of fans marched to Washington, for Pete's (as in Rozelle) sake.

A fundamental aspect of the passion that Clevelanders have for their sports teams is their desperation. They are diehard fans, many sadly dying hard, without the joy of ever having basked in a championship glow. Listen to any local radio sports talk show, and if the Browns lose a number of games in a row, one would think that nobody would show

A common sight in the Muny and Port lots before a Browns' game, pre-game tailgating has become legendary in Cleveland. *(Cleveland Public Library collection)*

up to the next home game. Judging by callers' comments, one would assume they had abandoned their team's sinking ship. But really, that's just the public face Cleveland fans put on to deal with their pain. On the outside, when things are bad, they vent the steam of Hades. The fact is, fans making these calls, frustrated and desperate, are looking for a little help in dealing with their feelings.

Take a look online, too, and you'll discover a host of websites and blogs devoted to sharing the pain. In the virtual world, one can find such blogs as "God Hates Cleveland Sports," "Wait 'Til Next Year," "The Mistake by the Lake Times," and "Cursed Cleveland." They provide a forum for the faithful and a place to share all the sport moments and passions. Online diehards vent frustrations, consider what might have been, make wild predictions of doom or glory (rarely anything in between), and basically express their pride in their predicament.

Mark Tollafield of Mentor said he grew up dreaming of the Indians being in contention in September. He wanted to experience what it would be like to be in a pennant race. "I could never let myself really believe that someday we could actually be in the World Series." He said that when the Indians made it to the Series in 1995, it was an "out of body" experience during which he simply slumped to the ground and cried.

After the disastrous seventh game of the 1997 World Series, Brian Cayne of University Heights, who had been watching it in his fraternity house at Ohio State University, lay frozen and numb in a fetal position for hours afterward.

Totally normal, right?

So what are the other hallmarks of this special group of people? It's profound

chapter 5: inner lives

This jarring LeBron James dunk and the reaction to it captures the intensity that Cavs' fans bring to their support of the phenom and the team that has seen an incredible resurgence in recent years. *(David Richard photo)*

loyalty. But this loyalty is quite different from that of other sports fans around the country. This allegiance has been born from four decades of championship-less ball. In Cleveland, faithfulness has sprouted from the earth like a well-spring of heartache. It has infected the Lake Erie water supply. It has made us, well, peculiar.

Seth Guren, of Mayfield, says he can't miss a game of any of the teams, lest they "find out about it."

John Butler, who grew up in Bay Village, cancelled his subscription to The *Plain Dealer* after the paper published an editorial that was sympathetic to Art Modell soon after he took the team to Baltimore. He has not renewed it since.

His brother Chris, when asked about loyalty, simply said, "it's everything." Some, like Michael Condelli, see devotion to the teams as a lifetime commitment. "When you're a hardcore fan, you're a fan for life, not for the season, for the week, or any other stretch. It's life."

No matter where Clevelanders go, no matter what they do, they remain loyal. An online fan known as "ThisisTFIS," a Seattle resident, said that when he lived in Africa, he would check the baseball standings for the Tribe in a

Cleveland fans are a devoted lot. In 1982, during the players' strike, these supporters made their way to Cincinnati to watch a Browns' replacement team battle the Bengals. The Browns won 34-0.
(Cleveland Stadium Corporation photo, Cleveland Landmarks Press collection)

month-old *Time* magazine that he could get in Kasongo.

As a coping mechanism in maintaining staunch loyalty for forgettable teams, many have resigned themselves to the idea that no Cleveland team will ever win a championship. David Savage, who grew up in the Greater Cleveland area and lived for years in Cleveland Heights, said, "I just don't let myself believe that they will win."

Jeff Richman of Highland Heights admits to now being a sports purist as a way of coping with bad to mediocre teams. "I never expect them to win. Now I like basketball for its own sake, and when they win, it's much more exciting."

Online, a fan known as "ArtGold" wrote that he simply appreciated being competitive and "not being left for dead by mid-season."

An Indians' fan online known as "TitoFrancona" expressed it this way:

"All I want Dolan, Shapiro and Wedge to do is get this team to the playoffs, whatever happens from there on, I can deal with."

For Joe Dailey of Avon Lake, being a Cleveland sports fan means "learning to live with disappointment." As a rabid Browns' fan, he said he "lives on every win for a week, and I cry on every loss for a week."

Dailey captured the civic pride that fuels the hope for the positive national attention that winning can bring. "I have an eternal hope of one day winning the Super Bowl just to bring the city into the national spotlight in any positive way," he said.

Some, like Bonni Berger of Beachwood, have come to a straightforward conclusion: Cleveland teams have been cursed. To her, the freak plays and injuries over the years have simply defied statistics, explanations, or reason. When LeCharles Bentley, a St. Ignatius graduate and much-

chapter 5: inner lives

Probably not wanting to miss a minute of the excitement he hopes for from the field, this fan ingeniously is well prepared to battle thirst. *(Ron Kuntz photo)*

heralded free agent acquisition in 2006, went down with a severe knee injury that left him on the sidelines for what would have been his first season, The *Plain Dealer* posed the question to fans: Are we cursed? It's no surprise that virtually everyone responded positively. It makes us feel better to say that.

Perhaps Cleveland fans are similar to fans of other teams, but when national media outlets come to town to cover a game, or when an individual athlete from one of the Cleveland squads merits national attention through interviews, Cleveland sports fans relish the moment. A case in point: Remember the great show the fans and the team put on the very first Monday night football game in 1970, when 85,703 jammed Cleveland Municipal Stadium and witnessed the Browns 31-21 triumph over the New York Jets.

Cleveland fans took heart when the broadcasters of the 2007 NBA championship series narrated the many disappointments suffered by those living on the North Shore. It was consoling to know that others recognized the depth of local pain.

It is safe to say that Cleveland fans know more heartache than any other fan base. Consequently, they have invented more coping strategies than fans of other teams. That is not to say that all those strategies have been *successful*.

On an online forum, an Indians fan identified as "allhailshapiro" responding to how he or she dealt with the near misses of the Tribe in the 90s, simply wrote, "I didn't. I completely broke down, and it is why I do my posting from a mental hospital."

"VATribe" wrote online one word to describe how he dealt with the near misses: "Budweiser."

surviving the drought: cleveland sports fans since 1964

Cleveland Browns Stadium, on the lakefront, can experience some tough winter playing conditions. Here it is snowing so hard that the ground crew has to sweep the field to reveal the yardage markers. Though the weather is foul and the team is mediocre at best, the Stadium is packed, a tribute to the spirit of Cleveland sports fans. *(Ron Kuntz photo)*

During the Indians' 1997 playoff run, Cleveland fans were emotionally drained as the underdog Tribe upset the powerful Yankees in the Division Series and then squeaked by the Orioles in the American League Championship Series in dramatic fashion. The *Plain Dealer* began to run front-page stories about the psychological toll the games were having on Cleveland fans.

One of the best headlines: "Games getting to Tribe fans: Cleveland Free Clinic sets up hotline to help people who are too emotionally involved with the fortunes of the Indians." By the time the World Series came and went, the stories had become regular installments of group therapy.

Surely the characteristics described above can be seen in other fan bases around the country. Probably true. But to what degree? It's a matter of debate. But there seems to be two conclusions that one can draw about Cleveland devotees.

First, while fans in other cities can point to their brethren as similar to the way Cleveland fans have been described, few can point to this reality: many other cities have hoards of people transplanted from around the U.S. In Cleveland, there are relatively fewer transplants, and the native-born Clevelanders who remain here connect more deeply to the city and its fortunes. It means that Cleveland

The next time a Cleveland sports team wins a championship, I will . . .
"look to the heavens and scream, "It's about *%&$-ing time," — Mark Tollafield, Mentor

chapter 5: inner lives

Although not unheard of, snow in April at the Jake can sometimes delay a game. It was so bad in April 2007, that Cleveland fans had to be content with having their first "home" games played in Milwaukee. *(Ron Kuntz photo)*

sports players and teams are like family to so many Greater Clevelanders.

"The attachments to the teams are deeper because their roots to the city are deeper," Pluto said. When he was a kid, he grew up hearing stories about Lou Boudreau and Larry Doby as much or more than about his own aunts and uncles.

"They were like family - my parents talked of them like a second family, and that's not true in other places." And it didn't matter that some of the players or the teams they cheered on were terrible.

"Those teams, those people represent nice moments in our family's history, and the fact that they were terrible makes the story even better, because we can say, 'the team stunk, the facilities stunk, and we loved it.'"

An Indians' fan online known as "tribenut" posted this: "The Indians are as much a part of my life as my family and, like family, no matter how angry or frustrated they make me I will always be there to root for them."

Kristy Nagel, 23, of Mentor, sees Cleveland sports fans in a similar vein. "There's something about the fans - outsiders can't believe the dedication here to our sports teams. The media here covers them so much, too - they seem to report less about Wall Street and crimes, and it seems that half the focus of the media in Cleveland is on sports."

Is it disappointing to be a Cleveland sports follower? "Being a Cleveland sports fan is the most fantastic thing in the world."

Chris Butler of Bay Village captured the familial draw of sports in Cleveland when he said, "Sports in Cleveland will continue to be a communing force among its citizens. It's so much less about the championship banners hanging from the

surviving the drought: cleveland sports fans since 1964

Wonder what is going on in this fan's inner life? Just another example of the diehard nature of Cleveland fans and the extent they go to show their enthusiasm. *(David Richard photo)*

rafters than the afternoons spent on the sofa with friends and family, collectively agonizing and cheering each play and turn of action; the moments when you find yourself in another town but spot the brown and orange jacket in the crowd and instantly know you have a friend in your midst; the ritual of shaping our weekends around big games."

Second, other fans simply cannot relate to the inner turmoil that the truth - and the outcomes of each season - has produced: no championships in 43 years.

While it has meant that Cleveland's devotees have developed creative coping mechanisms, the fact that they have had to, year in and year out, season after season, team to team, is unique. Who else but Cleveland sports fans can claim the rare combination, cultivated for more than 40 years, of passionate loyalty and frustrated hopes into a desperately dysfunctional family? They're our guys, our teams, our desperation, our heartbreaks.

We could not live without them, and that fact is our badge of honor.

surviving the drought
cleveland
and its sports fans
6

"It's not your fault. It's not your fault. It's not your fault."

— Sean Maguire, *Good Will Hunting*

Let's face it. While Cleveland fans comprise a special fraternity, our uniqueness is ultimately a paradox. If it weren't for the hellish last-minute losses, the long drought of winning seasons, the disappointing free agent busts, and the annual, desperate cries from fans throughout the region, Cleveland fans wouldn't be as special as they are. For 43 years Cleveland sports fans have experienced those disheartening moments. That's what makes Cleveland fans distinctive.

Would we be any different if the Browns had captured some Super Bowls in the late 1960s, when they regularly made the playoffs and were considered one of the teams to beat?

Or what about the Browns in the 1980s? What if Brian Sipe had spotted an open Dave Logan in the end zone against Oakland in the final moments of the 1981 playoff game? What if, on third and 18, the Browns didn't allow Elway to complete a 20-yard pass against a prevent defense in the 1986 AFC Championship game? What if Earnest Byner held onto the football in the 1987 AFC Championship game and Jermiah Castille faded into history as just another schlump?

Would we seem a little less desperate if Michael Jordan actually had been drafted by the Portland Trailblazers (who passed him up and chose Sam Bowie instead) and the Cavs didn't have to face him and the Bulls every year in their own division, and later in the conference playoffs?

And what if, by some chance, the major league baseball owners had not decided to cancel the remainder of the 1994 season, with the Tribe a game out of first place? And what if Jose Mesa didn't

surviving the drought: cleveland sports fans since 1964

The Cleveland skyline in 1954. The city became a national powerhouse on manufacturing and heavy industry that started to decline in the 1950s, right around the same time the Tribe started its decline. Few would have been able to predict that the Indians would not return to the World Series for another 41 years.
(Cleveland Landmarks Press Collection)

shake off Sandy Alomar's call in the ninth inning of game 7 of the 1997 World Series and finished the job against the Marlins? What then? Would we have a little bigger spring in our steps? Would we be less tortured than we are?

Probably, but it is what it is. The fact is none of those things happened, and Cleveland fans have no choice but to ponder their collective fate. Yet, what happened in these sports arenas is really only part of the influences that have shaped Clevelanders in recent years.

Consider a few trends that have coincided in the past 40 years or so. Cleveland as a metropolitan area, like other Rust Belt cities built on blue-collar labor and large-scale manufacturing, has gone through wrenching changes. Globalization and the lure of cheaper labor in the South and in other countries has devastated Cleveland's manufacturing base, forcing the community to deal with new economic realities such as struggling industries and out-migration of Greater Clevelanders to other areas.

In addition, like in other major cities, racial problems have vexed Cleveland. The Hough riots in 1966 left in their wake four dead and millions of dollars in property damage. Two years later, a shootout in Glenville between police and black militants left ten dead. Just seven months before that, Cleveland had made national

The next time a Cleveland sports team wins a championship, I will . . .
"suspect people will still joke about the Cuyahoga catching on fire," — Chris Butler, Bay Village

chapter 6: cleveland and its sports fans

Cleveland's manufacturing base has struggled over the last half century, as the Old National Castings building attests. *(James A. Toman photo, Cleveland Landmarks Press Collection)*

headlines because its citizens elected the first black mayor of any major city. But tensions and problems couldn't be quelled by the election of one man. The events of the late 1960s and the federal court's busing desegregation order in 1978 had a hand in producing a metropolitan area that is largely poor and black in the central city and mostly white and more economically stable in the suburbs. In many ways, Cleveland today is really the tale of two cities: its city core and its suburban and exurban shell.

Then there were those other events that put Cleveland on comedians' joke lists throughout the 1960s and 1970s. The Cuyahoga River caught fire in 1969 and caught national attention shortly thereafter. Although flames had lipped the surface of the river before, never had it received so much attention. Then there are the other ignominious events:

Mayor Ralph Perk's hair caught on fire while attempting to use a welder's torch at a ribbon-cutting ceremony. His wife made headlines when she turned down a request by then-First Lady Pat Nixon for dinner in favor of keeping her bowling night. In 1975, a study concluded that Cleveland was the nation's second worst in social and economic problems among 58 major metropolitan areas. And then when in 1978 the "Boy Mayor," 26-year-old Dennis Kucinich, decided to draw the line in the sand against big business in Cleveland, the City defaulted on its loans, the first major city to ever do so.

Throw into the mix that the Browns, during this same time frame, hit their worst string of losing seasons in franchise history, the Indians finished horribly year after year, and the Cavaliers limped along in their first decade as an expansion NBA team, you have the recipe for an appetizer

The new Cleveland Browns Stadium opened in 1999 on the site of the original Cleveland Municipal Stadium. While the new arena is not the old "Lady on the Lake," it is still a place for Clevelanders to get as rabid as they have always been when cheering on the brown and orange.
(James A. Toman photo, Cleveland Landmarks Press Collection)

of embarrassment with a main dish of inferiority complex.

But think about it: of the many distressing sporting events that did happen, how many did Clevelanders actually have a hand in creating?

True, Cleveland fans were the ones during the Beer Night in 1974 who jumped onto the baseball field at the end of the Indians-Rangers game. Because the fans were so drunk, the disturbance lasted only a few minutes before they were subdued, but it nonetheless tarnished the image of the city and its fans. It was downright ugly.

The same goes for the December 2001 Browns' game versus the Jaguars. The Cleveland fans who threw beer bottles and other dangerous objects completely embarrassed themselves and other Cleveland fans.

The large majority of the Cleveland faithful have been left to bear the burden of such shameful behavior.

Other than that, Clevelanders didn't choose to default on the City's loans, didn't make national headlines by throwing oil in the river (well, admittedly, this might be a stretch), didn't catch their hair on fire, didn't strap on football pads or put on basketball and baseball uniforms. They didn't lose the heartbreakers or let games slip away. Those things happened while Clevelanders squirmed in their seats, watched with dismay, and groaned.

One might think of Cleveland sports fans as the children of divorce. When a father or mother pulls the kids aside to give them the bad news that the relationship has hit such a difficult time that it can no longer continue, his or her first words are often, "It's nothing you did. It's not your fault." Of course, those words don't make the kids feel any better. But if you

chapter 6: cleveland and its sports fans

The 1990s saw a rebirth of downtown Cleveland, partially brought about by the development of the Gateway sports complex in the old Central Market district and the opening of the lakefront attractions, the Rock and Roll Hall of Fame and Museum and the Great Lakes Science Center. *(David Kachinko Photos)*

surviving the drought: cleveland sports fans since 1964

This picture sort of says it all for Cleveland in the 1970s: Cleveland Mayor Ralph Perk (1972-1977) tosses out the first pitch in a largely empty Cleveland Municipal Stadium. For the Tribe during the 1970s, attendance only reached the million mark twice. *(Janet Macoska photo, Western Reserve Historical Society collection)*

were to examine much of Cleveland sports history and all its attendant miseries, one can reach a reasonable conclusion: Very little of what has happened has been the fault of the average Clevelander.

Go ahead. Repeat after me: "It's not our fault."

The tragic part about Cleveland's nadir was that Greater Clevelanders didn't have the option of filing for divorce from area leaders. Let's just say that would have created a massive legal issue - who would take custody of the metropolitan area's three million souls who had been shaken to the core by so many failings?

All of this is made worse when one considers the fact that Cleveland, in the century before 1964, was one of the great American success stories. It boomed on industry from the Civil War, became the place where immigrants from around the globe flocked to find jobs, was the home of the wealthiest man in the U.S. - John D. Rockefeller - and one of the most celebrated mayors in U.S. history - Tom L. Johnson. At its height, it was a model of progressive governance and planning. It was the fifth largest city in the nation, with one of the most interesting and diverse mixes of people. It was home to national political conventions, a burgeoning real estate empire controlled by the two reclusive Van Sweringen brothers, and to one of the most beautiful streets (Euclid Avenue) in

The next time a Cleveland sports team wins a championship, I will . . .

"hope to be there. Hell, I'm 78 and I hope they make it soon," — Kenny Konz (former Brown defensive back from 1953-59), Alliance

chapter 6: cleveland and its sports fans

Although the 1970s did not bring much joy to Tribe fans, there were great moments. New player-manager Frank Robinson doffs his cap to the fans on opening day 1974. A few minutes later he blasted a homerun in first at-bat as an Indian, a feat fans voted the all-time greatest Tribe thrill. *(Janet Macoska photo, Western Reserve Historical Society collection)*

the nation. It became known as a center of culture with a museum of art the envy of other cities and with an internationally renowned orchestra.

And in sports, Cleveland teams won championships. The Tribe did it twice (1920 and 1948), and came close throughout the 1950s. The Browns emerged as a perennial NFL powerhouse in the late 1940s, 1950s, and 1960s. The football team captured three championships in the 1950s and made it to the premier game four other times, and then upset the vaunted Baltimore Colts in the 1964 NFL Championship game. During that span, the Browns racked up a brawny .728 winning percentage.

But Cleveland in the last few decades has fallen far from its once proud position.

Throw in the explosion of the media over that same time period, and it has made matters worse. Professional sports as businesses and entertainment attractions have become multi-billion-dollar enterprises. Big-time money. While sports before the 1960s were popular, that era cannot compare to more recent times. The flood of media outlets has produced an ever greater profusion of sports television shows, networks, newspapers, magazines, and internet sites.

This last development cannot be overstated. Cities, as a result of such overwhelming media attention in sports, have

surviving the drought: cleveland sports fans since 1964

Cleveland can always be counted on to put on a real show. Cleveland has hosted All-Star games five times and holds the top three slots for all-time best attendance. The fifth game, the first played in Jacobs Field, came in 1997. The event was a sellout. *(Janet Macoska photo, Western Reserve Historical Society collection)*

in a significant way come to be defined by what happens in the sports arena. And in virtually no other arena can cities (or their representatives) compete more simply and directly than in sports. And in practically no other medium can that competition be more starkly relayed than on television.

Take, for instance, Pittsburgh. Although it has experienced the same wrenching changes as other Rust Belt cities, its citizens were lucky - that's right, Pittsburgh fans, you had nothing to do with any of it - enough to smooth over the economic and demographic realities with glorious Super Bowl runs in the 1970s and other sporadic successes in baseball and hockey. Because of those championship moments, Pittsburgh fans have been able, at least intermittently, to forget the fact that their city, like Cleveland, is struggling and one that needs to reinvent itself in a sea of change. One could argue that

the rabid Pittsburgh fans are as much a product of their struggling circumstances as those from Cleveland - their collective identity forged by the teams that fought in the sports arenas. When those teams succeeded, Pittsburghers could tell themselves they were OK. They were champions. Even though they actually weren't - the teams they cheered for were.

Sorry, Pittsburgh fans. When you are tempted to gloat in the championships that you have been lucky enough to enjoy, think of it in this way. You are like a child born into wealth. You are fortunate. Cleveland fans, on the other hand, are like children born into poverty. Do Pittsburghers think it's appropriate to make fun of poor kids? Perhaps.

So Cleveland has gone through its longest period without a championship at a time when the confluence of major trends spelled problems. Throw all of

chapter 6: cleveland and its sports fans

At the 1997 All-Star Game, a packed house, a Major League party, a resurgent downtown Cleveland, and a playoff-bound team had most Cleveland fans feeling tremendous energy.
(Janet Macoska photo, Western Reserve Historical Society collection)

these things into the mix, and Cleveland has struggled to forge a new identity and feel a renewed civic pride.

No wonder Clevelanders bring a mix of desperation and urgency to their sports teams. In this new era, sports have become the visible definition of entire cities – fairly or not.

While Cleveland's economy continues to struggle in post-industrial America, Cleveland fans can hold their heads high. They have left an indelible mark on the rest of the nation. Cleveland fans have been able to demonstrate an impressive – perhaps even incredible – devotion to their teams that has turned heads in the sporting world. Cleveland fans in the 1980s took the idea of the Dawg Pound and made it the talk of the NFL world as a place where undying loyalty and manic dedication to the Browns collided in a fury of pure passion. When Browns' owner Art Modell moved the team to Baltimore and Browns' fans marched to Washington to protest the move, and commentators around the country spoke of the raw deal that had befallen Cleveland Browns' fans, citing them as some of the best in the nation. Word is, too, that the Browns Backers, groups of Browns fans in major cities around the world, are the largest collective fan group in the world. During the impressive Indians' seasons from 1994 to 2001 fans sold out Jacobs Field a record 455 straight times, a feat unmatched in Major League Baseball.

So, in these last decades of championship-less competition, Cleveland fans have truly become an icon of faithful devotion. The typical Cleveland sports fan is now lauded for displaying undying loyalty, passionate fervor, and desperate hope.

Former Browns' lineman Dick Shafrath, who played with the team

surviving the drought: cleveland sports fans since 1964

Tribe designated hitter Travis Hafner is pensive as he prepares to enter the on-deck circle. The slugger has been a major weapon in the Tribe's arsenal since 2003, and fans have high hopes for him and the rest of the Tribe. *(Ron Kuntz photo)*

from 1959-1971 and suited up for the last Cleveland team to win a championship, has been struck since his playing days by the loyalty of the fans.

"The fans here live it and die it," he said. "They pass it on from generation to generation, and I've never met more loyal people than in Cleveland."

Same goes for Bingo Smith, one of the most popular players to ever don a Cavaliers' jersey.

"Once you're a sports figure here, the fans don't forget you," Smith said. "That doesn't happen too often. Here, the fans are unique because even if you don't win a championship, if they know you're doing the best you can, they still come out to support you. Even if you come up short, they're still there for you."

Sam Rutigliano, who just recently moved back to the Cleveland area, echoed Smith.

"[Cleveland fans] are the flagship of the fleet," he said. "Every year, Cleveland proves what an unbelievably loyal and rabid fan base it has." Rutigliano came back because he has always had an attachment to Cleveland. "I came back not to take any bows, just to be here. It's just so much fun to be here," he said.

He is regularly overwhelmed with Cleveland sports fans and impressed with their devotion.

The next time a Cleveland sports team wins a championship, I will . . .
"hope that I won't celebrate it by banging my head on the inside of my coffin," — Harvey Morrison, University Heights

chapter 6: cleveland and its sports fans

Cavaliers owner Dan Gilbert, seemingly looking to the Almighty for a little assistance in getting the Cavs a championship, is actually only checking out the scoreboard at the Q. His purchase of the franchise, combined with the arrival of LeBron James, has sparked renewed hope through the Greater Cleveland area. *(Ron Kuntz photo)*

"I recently went to speak in Newport News, Virginia, and Cleveland fans were there, asking me for my autograph." He once took a vacation to New Zealand and was in Auckland when some guy asked him about Red Right 88. "Tell me, what other sports franchise has that?

"One of the very strong things that they identify with is the audacity of hope," Rutigliano said. "The thing they hang onto is what Paul Brown built and the great tradition of the Cleveland Browns. They hold on to that dearly, and it's so far inside everybody that it will never, ever change."

Cleveland sports fans speak of many things when considering their own loyalty. For fans like B.J. Robb of Hudson, it's about taking a beating every year and before Browns' home games showing up with his neighbor at bars like the Blind Pig in the Warehouse District to bond and get excited, even when the Browns aren't winning.

For long-time fans like Bruce Hoffman from Stow or William Gresham from Cleveland Heights, loyalty stems from the winning traditions of the teams in the 1950s and 1960s.

"The atmosphere and tradition of those years has kept me coming back," said Hoffman. His loyalty keeps him hoping to relive that greatness again.

For others like Bob Nilsen of Twinsburg, loyalty as a Cleveland sports fan is fairly simple. "It beats the hell out of being a loyal New Orleans fan."

Chris Stupica of Hudson summed up his pride in Cleveland fans' loyalty. "I've lived in different parts of the country, and it's easy to be a Pittsburgh or a New England fan in football. They have legacies of championships. But to keep coming back, year after year, knowing you're probably going to get your heart broken, that's true loyalty."

Formar Browns' quarterback Charlie Frye, the University of Akron star who grew up idolizing Bernie Kosar and then got a chance to live his dream by donning the brown and orange, said in a *Plain Dealer* interview that he thinks about the fact that Cleveland fans have experienced years of heartbreak and yet they show an undying love for the professional teams in the area. "It would be great to bring a championship to Cleveland. The fans deserve it," he said.

Do Cleveland fans deserve it more than, say, San Diego fans? Or any other fans in the country? That's a tough question to answer, but if one considers whether or not Cleveland fans are most worthy of a championship, take a moment to think about the millions of Cleveland fans who have been there physically, or psychologically, or emotionally, for the Cavs, Browns, and Indians since 1964.

Think of the hoards of souls who have braved bone-chilling Lake Erie winds or toughed out Tribe games in early spring rain at the Jake or at old Cleveland Municipal Stadium, traveled back and forth from the snowy Coliseum or the Gund or the Q even when the games were over by halftime. Think of the millions of fans who have had to endure insults from Pittsburghers, who, living only two hours away, bask in their city's numerous championships. Did the football gods do this on purpose - put the team with the most Super Bowl rings two hours away from one of only five football teams who have never even reached the big show?

Think of the hoards of Cleveland fans who watched titles slip away, whose hopes were dashed and hearts shredded.

Think of the countless fans who have been born since 1964 and have grown up idolizing teams and players and actually believe that, finally, this year would be the year.

Think of the thousands of callers who have weighed in on sports talk shows, who have argued with Pete Franklin, Mike Trivisonno, or Bruce Drennan, who have devoured pre-season sports magazines, Monday morning sports pages, and dozens of books on Cleveland sports moments. Think of the Clevelanders who have set aside a room in their home as a shrine to their team and who decorate it with every possible display of team devotion. Think of the fans who have painted their faces and chests, who tailgate like it's their hobby.

When one considers them all, one wonders - are we an exceptional fraternity? Is it true, that nobody, nobody, could understand what it's like to be a Cleveland sports fan? To go from exhilarating highs to gut-wrenching lows, and to still be a group without its ultimate wish – a championship?

The answer, clearly, is yes. Cleveland sports fans are distinctive in relation to other fans, mainly because the circumstances over the last four decades (and counting) have made them crazy.

And so here is the ultimate question for Cleveland fans. They can look at the current miserable state of championship-less sports and consider: Would we rather be a special, unique bunch of fans who bring a mix of desperation, allegiance, and passion to our teams, or would we rather be like the other more common groups of fans from almost any other major league city who have savored the title of "champion"?

Actually, don't answer that question.

chapter 6: cleveland and its sports fans

LeBron James begins to take the floor in a 2007 playoff game in typical fashion - with outstretched arms greeting fans' adoration. *(David Richard photo)*

references

Brown, Gerry, and Michael Morrison. 2007.
ESPN Sports Almanac 2007.
Lake Worth, FL: ESPN Books.

Cleveland Browns 2006 Media Guide. 2006.
Cleveland: The Cleveland Browns.

Cleveland Indians Media Guide 2007. 2007.
Cleveland: The Cleveland Indians.

Dyer, Bob. 2003.
Cleveland Sports Legends: The 20 Most Glorious and Gut-Wrenching Moments of All Time.
Cleveland: Gray & Co. Publishers.

Huler, Scott. 1999.
On Being Brown.
Cleveland: Gray & Company Publishers.

Keim, John. 1999.
Legends by the Lake: The Cleveland Browns at Municipal Stadium.
Akron: The University of Akron Press.

Knight, Jonathan. 2003.
Kardiac Kids: The Story of the 1980 Cleveland Browns.
Kent, OH: Kent State University Press.

Long, Tim. 1996.
Browns Memories.
Cleveland: Gray & Co. Publishers.

Long, Tim, and Don Fox. 1997.
Indians Memories.
Cleveland: Gray & Co. Publishers.

Menzer, Joe, and Burt Graeff. 1994.
Cavs from Fitch to Fratello.
Champaign, IL: Sagamore Publishing.

Pluto, Terry. 1994.
The Curse of Rocky Colavito.
New York: Simon & Schuster.

Pluto, Terry. 2004.
False Start.
Cleveland: Gray & Company Publishers

Poplar, Michael. 1997.
Fumble! The Browns, Modell, and the Move.
Cleveland: Cleveland Landmarks Press.

Queenan, Joe. 2003.
True Believers: The Tragic Inner Lives of Sports Fans.
New York: Henry Holt and Company.

Schneider, Russell. 1999.
The Best of the Cleveland Browns Memories: Players, Coaches, and Games.
Cleveland: Moonlight Publishing.

Toman, James. and Gregory Deegan. 1997.
Cleveland Stadium: The Last Chapter.
Cleveland: Cleveland Landmarks Press.

media

Bleeding Orange and Brown: A Cleveland Tradition
(directed, produced, edited by Christopher Pete, Jeffrey Haynes, Good Idea Bad Idea Production,) 2005.

sources

periodicals

The *Plain Dealer*
    April 17, 1965
    April 4, 1966
    September 2, 1984
    April 5 - 6, 1987
    November 4, 1988
    November 3, 1989
    November 5, 1992
    October 7 - 29, 1997

The *New York Times*
    April 5, 1987
    September 13, 1987
    November 6, 1992

Sports Illustrated
    September 5, 1984
    January 8, 1987
    January 15, 1987
    November 9, 1987
    August 29, 1988
    November 7, 1988
    Fall 1989
    September 1989
    November 6, 1989
    November 5, 1990
    November 11, 1991
    November 9, 1992
    September 4, 1995
    April 1, 1996
    Playoff Preview 1997
    October 27, 1997
    March 23, 1998

The *Sporting News*
    January 9, 1965
    September 18, 1965
    September 17, 1966
    September 15, 1967
    January 6, 1968
    April 13, 1968
    September 14, 1968
    September 3, 1984
    January 12, 1987
    April 1, 1987
    April 1, 1988
    November 1, 1988
    September 1, 1988
    January 16, 1995
    February 13, 1995
    April 1, 1996